Diseases and Disorders

Measles and Rubella

Titles in the Diseases and Disorders series include:

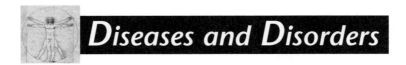
Diseases and Disorders

Measles
and Rubella

by Barbara Saffer

LUCENT BOOKS
A part of Gale, Cengage Learning

GALE
CENGAGE Learning™

Detroit • New York • San Francisco • New Haven, Conn • Waterville, Maine • London

© 2006 Gale, a part of Cengage Learning

For more information, contact
Lucent Books
27500 Drake Rd.
Farmington Hills, MI 48331-3535
Or you can visit our Internet site at gale.cengage.com

LIBRARY OF CONGRESS CATALOGING-IN-PUBLICATION DATA

Saffer, Barbara.
   Measles and rubella / by Barbara Saffer.
     p. cm. — (Diseases and disorders series)
   Includes bibliographical references and index.
   ISBN 1-59018-410-6 (hardcover : alk. paper)
     1. Measles—Juvenile literature. 2. Rubella—Juvenile literature. I. Title. II. Series.
RA644.M5S24 2005
614.5'23—dc22

                                                2005012875

Printed in the United States of America
4 5 6 7 12 11 10 09 08

Table of Contents

"The Most Difficult Puzzles Ever Devised"

CHARLES BEST, ONE of the pioneers in the search for a cure for diabetes, once explained what it is about medical research that intrigued him so. "It's not just the gratification of knowing one is helping people," he confided, "although that probably is a more heroic and selfless motivation. Those feelings may enter in, but truly, what I find best is the feeling of going toe to toe with nature, of trying to solve the most difficult puzzles ever devised. The answers are there somewhere, those keys that will solve the puzzle and make the patient well. But how will those keys be found?"

Since the dawn of civilization, nothing has so puzzled people—and often frightened them, as well—as the onset of illness in a body or mind that had seemed healthy before. A seizure, the inability of a heart to pump, the sudden deterioration of muscle tone in a small child—being unable to reverse such conditions or even to understand why they occur was unspeakably frustrating to healers. Even before there were names for such conditions, even before they were understood at all, each was a reminder of how complex the human body was, and how vulnerable.

While our grappling with understanding diseases has been frustrating at times, it has also provided some of humankind's most heroic accomplishments. Alexander Fleming's accidental discovery in 1928 of a mold that could be turned into penicillin has resulted in the saving of untold millions of lives. The isolation of the enzyme insulin has reversed what was once a death sentence for anyone with diabetes. There have been great strides in combating conditions for which there is not yet a cure, too. Medicines can help AIDS patients live longer, diagnostic tools such as mammography and ultrasounds can help doctors find tumors while they are treatable, and laser surgery techniques have made the most intricate, minute operations routine.

This "toe-to-toe" competition with diseases and disorders is even more remarkable when seen in a historical continuum. An astonishing amount of progress has been made in a very short time. Just two hundred years ago, the existence of germs as a cause of some diseases was unknown. In fact, it was less than 150 years ago that a British surgeon named Joseph Lister had difficulty persuading his fellow doctors that washing their hands before delivering a baby might increase the chances of a healthy delivery (especially if they had just attended to a diseased patient)!

Each book in Lucent's Diseases and Disorders series explores a disease or disorder and the knowledge that has been accumulated (or discarded) by doctors through the years. Each book also examines the tools used for pinpointing a diagnosis, as well as the various means that are used to treat or cure a disease. Finally, new ideas are presented—techniques or medicines that may be on the horizon.

Frustration and disappointment are still part of medicine, for not every disease or condition can be cured or prevented. But the limitations of knowledge are being pushed outward constantly; the "most difficult puzzles ever devised" are finding challengers every day.

Persistent Childhood Diseases

BEFORE THE DEVELOPMENT of vaccines, children throughout the world commonly suffered from a series of diseases characterized by conspicuous skin rashes. These illnesses include measles, rubella, scarlet fever, Duke's disease, fifth disease, and roseola. In recent years, medical advances and childhood vaccination have greatly reduced the occurrence of these diseases, especially in developed nations. Measles and rubella, however, have persisted in developing countries and continue to cause serious concern worldwide.

Measles, also called rubeola, is best known for the blotchy red rash it causes. However, since measles begins as an infection of the respiratory tract, symptoms of the disease include a runny nose, a cough, fever, red eyes, and fatigue. The *Morbillivirus* microbes that cause measles are disseminated by way of respiratory secretions spewed from the mouth and nose of a measles sufferer. The virus is extremely infectious and spreads readily. Referring to the ease of disseminating measles viruses, a report from the Oregon Department of Human Services notes that, "Measles is so contagious that two or three minutes spent in an ER [emergency room] or doctor's office waiting room may be sufficient to infect people who pass through the same room hours later."[1]

Though many people may think of measles as a relatively harmless childhood malady, the disease can be deadly. In fact, measles has been called one of the greatest killers of children in history. Even today, measles slays more children than any other vaccine-preventable disease. Most measles deaths result from complications associated with the illness, such as severe diarrhea, pneumonia (inflammation of the lungs), or encephalitis (inflammation of the brain). Even people who recover from measles may suffer severe complications such as blindness, deafness, and mental retardation. A vaccine that protects people against measles has been available since 1963. Immunization with the vaccine has reduced the incidence of measles in many countries.

This child is suffering from chicken pox, one of several serious diseases, including measles and rubella, that can cause a severe skin rash.

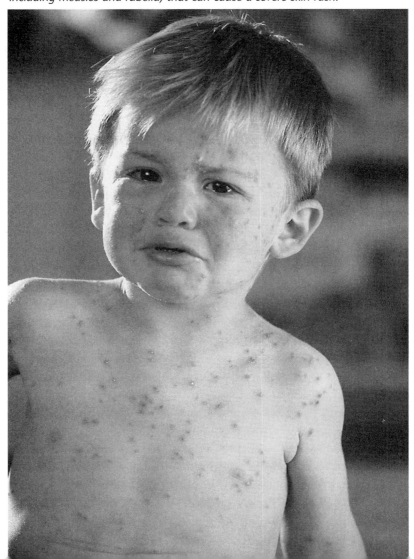

Measles Deaths in the United States, 1912–1982

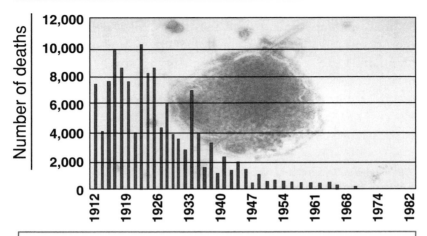

Number of deaths

12,000
10,000
8,000
6,000
4,000
2,000
0

1912 1919 1926 1933 1940 1947 1954 1961 1968 1974 1982

Better public health awareness by the 1930s helped dramatically reduce deaths caused by measles. But it was not until the licensing of the measles vaccine in 1963 and the MMR (Measles-Mumps-Rubella) vaccine in 1971 that nearly zero deaths occured in the United States.

Nevertheless, measles still infects 40 to 50 million people each year, killing close to 1 million victims, mostly in developing regions where access to medicine is limited.

Though it often causes a rash similar to that of measles, rubella, also known as German measles, is generally a mild disease. Like measles viruses, the *Rubivirinae* viruses that cause rubella are spread by way of respiratory droplets. People with rubella typically exhibit a low-grade fever, swollen glands, and a fine pink rash. Rubella symptoms may be so inconspicuous, though, that they go unnoticed, particularly in children. If a pregnant woman becomes ill with rubella, however, the consequences may be devastating. During the early stages of pregnancy, the rubella virus can infect the developing infant and cause serious birth defects. These defects, collectively known as congenital rubella syndrome (CRS), may include blindness, deafness, heart defects, mental retardation, and other serious afflictions.

A vaccine to protect people against rubella has been available since 1969. Use of the vaccine has greatly reduced the incidence of rubella in the industrialized world. In developing parts of the world, however, rubella vaccination rates remain low, primarily due to lack of financial resources. In these regions, the possibility remains high that pregnant women will contract rubella and give birth to infants with CRS.

Local medical agencies in most countries, as well as international health organizations such as the World Health Organization (WHO) and the March of Dimes, strongly promote measles and rubella inoculations. Most health departments use a combination vaccine, called MMR (measles-mumps-rubella) vaccine, which provides protection against measles, rubella, and mumps. (Mumps is a contagious viral disease that affects the parotid, or salivary, glands.) The short-term goal of health authorities is to reduce the number of deaths from measles and to lessen the number of children born with CRS. Speaking of the possibility of eradicating CRS, Dr. Michael Katz, senior vice president for research and global programs of the March of Dimes, observed, "Universal immunization of infants [with rubella vaccine], coupled with 'catch up' immunization of adolescents and women of childbearing age who did not receive the vaccine as infants, can eliminate congenital rubella syndrome."[2] Medical experts such as Katz hope that, over time, stringent worldwide immunization against measles and rubella will erase these diseases from the globe.

Chapter 1

The History of Measles and Rubella

E PIDEMIC DISEASES HAVE afflicted humanity since ancient times. Some plagues, like the Black Death (bubonic plague), were so devastating that they were written about by many early scholars. Thus, it is easy to chart the path of destruction they caused. Other illnesses, such as measles, rubella, smallpox, and scarlet fever, have also been documented in historical texts. However, because these rash-causing diseases were often confused with one another, it is more difficult to trace their dispersal.

Measles in the Ancient World

Many human illnesses, including measles, influenza, malaria, smallpox, and pertussis, arose from germs that originally infected animals. When humans domesticated wild creatures, such as sheep, goats, pigs, cows, horses, and camels, disease-causing microbes that normally infected the animals mutated, or changed, to infect people. Scientists believe that the measles virus, which is closely related to viruses that cause distemper in dogs and rinderpest in cattle, originated in this fashion. In fact, scientists believe the measles virus probably arose from rinderpest or a similar virus.

To thrive, measles must be passed directly from one person to another. Historically, therefore, measles required a population of at least ten thousand people living close together to become entrenched in human communities. Anthropologists believe, therefore, that measles became a common human disease in about 2500 B.C. when ancient cities in Mesopotamia (a region in what is now Iraq) grew populous enough to allow the disease to take hold.

From its origin in the Middle East, measles was dispersed to other populated regions. In A.D. 165 Roman soldiers fighting in Mesopotamia were forced to retreat when an epidemic, probably measles or smallpox, struck the troops. Upon their return to Italy, the soldiers spread the disease across the Roman empire with dire results. The epidemic killed one-quarter to one-third of affected populations in the Mediterranean region.

In A.D. 162 an epidemic like that in the Roman empire, also thought to be measles or smallpox, occurred among Chinese warriors fighting nomadic barbarian tribes. The disease killed about one-third of the Chinese soldiers. In A.D. 310 another such epidemic struck northwestern China, killing most victims of the disease. Soon afterward, in A.D. 322, a third epidemic of measles

Epidemics have spread illness and death for centuries. This engraving depicts an outbreak of bubonic plague in Greece in the fourteenth century.

or smallpox killed about one-quarter of the Chinese population over a much larger area.

Historical records indicate that measles repeatedly broke out in many other early societies. For example, measles is thought to have struck Athens, Greece, in 430 B.C.; Japan in A.D. 552; and England, Ireland, and Wales in A.D. 664. In the eighth century, invading Muslim Saracens from North Africa spread measles across the Iberian Peninsula (Portugal and Spain) and into France. Many early societies recognized that some diseases were contagious, and therefore caregivers often isolated sick individuals to prevent the spread. Nevertheless, infectious diseases such as measles and smallpox continued to devastate populations in Europe and elsewhere.

Rhazes Distinguishes Measles from Smallpox

Measles and smallpox were confused by ancient physicians because the early symptoms of both diseases, such as headache, fever, and flat red spots on the skin, are similar. The first doctor to clearly differentiate the two illnesses was Abu Bakr Muhammad ibn Zakariya ar-Razi, also known to Europeans as Rhazes of Baghdad (the capital of modern-day Iraq).

Rhazes, who lived from about A.D. 865 to 925, was a Persian physician who became chief of the Baghdad hospital. Considered one of the greatest medical authorities of his time, Rhazes wrote many books about health and disease. These volumes, later translated into Latin, French, Italian, Hebrew, and Greek, were used in Western and Eastern medical schools for hundreds of years. In one of Rhazes's books, titled *Al-Judari wa al-Hasbah* (*A Treatise on Smallpox and Measles*), the eminent physician concluded that measles and smallpox were distinct diseases. He based this on his observation of the symptoms that accompany the two diseases. In *Al-Judari wa al-Hasbah*, Rhazes wrote,

> The eruption [rash] . . . is preceded by a continued fever, pain in the back, itching in the nose, and terrors in sleep . . . also a pricking which the patient feels all over his body; a fullness of the face . . . an inflamed color, and vehement redness in both the cheeks; a

redness of both the eyes; a heaviness of the whole body; great un-
easiness, the symptoms of which are stretching and yawning; a
pain in the throat and chest, with a slight difficulty in breathing,
and cough . . . pain and heaviness of the head; inquietude, distress
of mind, nausea, and anxiety . . . and especially an intense redness
of the gums. . . . When, therefore, you see these symptoms, or
some of the worst of them (such as the pain of the back, and the
terrors in sleep with the continued fever) then you may be as-
sured that the eruption of one or other of these diseases [measles
or smallpox] in the patient is nigh at hand; except that there is not
in the measles so much pain of the back as in the smallpox, nor in
the smallpox so much anxiety and nausea as in the measles.[3]

While Rhazes realized there were differences between smallpox and measles, he mistakenly believed that measles was a variety of smallpox. Thus, Rhazes speculated that both diseases
had the same cause. This erroneous belief was not dispelled for
hundreds of years. By the early 1600s, however, most physicians
recognized that measles and smallpox were separate diseases.
Historical records do not indicate exactly when and how the two
diseases were differentiated, but by 1629 London's annual "bills
of mortality" (lists of people who died and the causes of death)
recorded measles and smallpox separately.

Rhazes called measles *hasbah*, which means "eruption" in Ara-
bic. By the fourteenth century, the disease had acquired the name
measles. The derivation of the term, however, is not clear. Some
historians think the word *measles* came from the Middle English
mesel, which meant "leper", or the Latin word *misellus*, which referred to a wretched person. Other scholars believe the term
measles came from the Middle English *maselen*, which means "little spots." In any case, measles eventually became the most common name for the illness in the Western world.

Measles Epidemics Devastate New World Natives

During the Middle Ages and the Renaissance, measles epidemics
broke out frequently in Europe and Asia. As with most illnesses,
people who recuperated from measles generally became immune

Rhazes

Born in Rayy, Persia (now Iran), in A.D. 865, Rhazes was among the most accomplished men of his time. A talented musician and singer in his youth, Rhazes went on to study astronomy, chemistry, mathematics, philosophy, and medicine. After becoming a celebrated physician, Rhazes headed the Royal Hospital in Rayy. He later moved to a similar position at the famous Muqtadari Hospital in Baghdad, Iraq. As a medical teacher, Rhazes attracted students from all across Asia. He also traveled widely, providing medical treatment to rulers and princes as well as ordinary people. Rhazes was said to be compassionate, kind, virtuous, and devoted to the service of his patients.

Rhazes was a pioneer in many areas of medicine. He was the first doctor to distinguish between measles and smallpox; to treat pediatrics as a separate field of medicine; to link allergies, such as hay fever, with the scent of roses; and to use music as a healing aid. He also wrote early medical treatises about kidney stones, intestinal pain, and joint maladies. Rhazes wrote more than two hundred books about medicine, chemistry, and philosophy. His medical encyclopedia, *Kitab al-Hawi fi al-tibb* (*The Comprehensive Book on Medicine*), was translated into many languages and earned him enduring fame.

to the disease. Over time, therefore, most adults in affected regions were measles survivors and resistant to the virus. Measles then became a childhood illness in those areas. Measles was first referred to as a childhood disease in Europe in 1224. By the 1700s measles had become a leading cause of death among children, and one of the most feared diseases in the world.

While many European and Asian adults had grown immune to measles and other diseases, their New World counterparts were not so lucky. Furthermore, when Europeans arrived in North and South America, they brought numerous contagious diseases with them. For example, when the Spanish explorer and conqueror Hernando Cortés landed in Mexico in 1519, his crew soon infected the native Aztec people with measles, smallpox, and other illnesses. Because New World populations had not been exposed to these sicknesses previously, adults and children had no immunity and succumbed readily. As additional explorers and colonists arrived in the New World, they spread many Old World infectious diseases across the Americas, including bubonic plague, cholera, malaria, diphtheria, mumps, pleurisy, scarlet fever, pneumonia, typhoid fever, pertussis, yellow fever, syphilis, smallpox, and measles. Bernardino Vázquez de Tapia, who was with Cortés when he conquered Mexico, reported on the devastation inflicted on the Aztecs by diseases. "The pestilence of measles and smallpox was so severe and cruel that more than one-fourth of the Indian people in all the land died," observes Vázquez de Tapia, "and this

Hernando Cortés and other European explorers brought measles and other diseases to the native populations of the New World.

loss had the effect of hastening the end of the fighting because there died a great quantity of men and warriors and many lords and captains and valiant men against whom we would have had to fight and deal with as enemies."[4] Though the Aztecs were fairly knowledgeable about health and sickness, they quickly succumbed to European diseases. Like many other early civilizations, the Aztecs attributed diseases to magical or supernatural causes like sorcerers and gods. Aztec medical treatment, therefore, included a mixture of religion, magic, and science. As with other civilizations that lacked advanced medical treatments, however, Aztec practices could not stop the measles plague.

Accounts of early epidemics among natives of the New World are sketchy. However, records indicate that measles outbreaks decimated native populations in Central America and Mexico from 1531 to 1533. From there the disease spread to North America, where it struck Native American tribes again and again. The spread of the diseases was abetted by European colonization of North America in the early sixteenth century. The result of contact with the colonists was in many ways disastrous. Historical records note at least seven measles epidemics among Native American populations between 1633 and 1788.

With no protection, Native Americans fell victim to the disease in huge numbers. Historians speculate that, by the beginning of the twentieth century, epidemic diseases and other hardships had wiped out about 90 percent of Native American populations. By then, however, most surviving Native American adults were immune to measles, and as had occurred elsewhere, measles became a childhood disease in their communities.

Measles in the Colonies

Measles also affected European colonists in America. Between 1657 and 1788, a total of nine measles outbreaks occurred in white settlements in Massachusetts, Connecticut, New York, Pennsylvania, and South Carolina. There were few trained doctors in the colonies and only a handful of hospitals. Thus, colonists were ill-prepared to deal with measles epidemics, and many died. The Reverend Cotton Mather of Boston's Old North

Church, best remembered for encouraging the Salem witch trials, suffered grievous losses during a measles epidemic in 1713. Within a twelve-day period, Mather lost his wife, three children, including newborn twins, and a devoted maid. Devastated by the epidemic, Mather observed that it was "a very heavy calamity, a malady grievous to most, mortal to many, and leaving pernicious [deadly] relics behind it all."[5] Eventually, however, as in other places, many colonists gained immunity to the disease, and measles became a childhood disease in the American settlements.

Medical Discoveries Foster Greater Understanding of the Diseases

While centuries of measles outbreaks had shown that the disease was infectious, the contagious nature of the illness was not explicitly proven until the eighteenth century. In 1757 Francis Home, a physician in Edinburgh, Scotland, used the blood of measles victims to transmit the disease to uninfected individuals. Home developed a measles vaccine, but his methodology did not ensure a high success rate for prevention. Nearly a century later, in 1846, the renowned Danish physician Peter Panum studied a measles outbreak in the Faeroe Islands, between Iceland and England. Panum demonstrated that the illness readily spread through the air from person to person and island to island. These discoveries did nothing, however, to aid the tens of thousands who fell victim to an outbreak in England and Wales between 1838 and 1840.

Although measles could not be countered in the nineteenth century, scientists were learning more about infectious diseases. In the 1860s the French scientist Louis Pasteur proved that germs cause disease and that the spread of germs resulted in epidemics. Pasteur also demonstrated that every disease is caused by a specific microbe; he then went on to identify three bacteria, a type of microbe, that cause human illnesses: *Streptococcus*, which causes strep throat; *Staphylococcus*, which causes boils; and *Pneumococcus*, which causes pneumonia. Measles, however, was not caused by a bacteria; it was caused by a virus. Viruses were first discovered

Louis Pasteur

Louis Pasteur, called the father of microbiology, was born in Dole, France, in 1822. He graduated from the Royal College of Besançon in 1842 with honors in mathematics, physics, Latin, and drawing. Pasteur continued his studies at the École Normale Supérieure in Paris, where he trained to be a chemistry professor.

In 1856, while Pasteur was an academic in Lille, a distiller asked him to investigate why his beers and wines sometimes went sour. Pasteur learned that microbes were responsible for fermenting sugar into alcohol and that sour alcoholic beverages contained different microbes than good alcoholic beverages. Pasteur also proved that mild heating could kill the unwanted microbes and prevent souring. This process came to be called pasteurization, and was later used to prevent spoilage of milk and other foods.

Pasteur went on to demonstrate that numerous infectious diseases, including chicken cholera, rabies, anthrax, and pneumonia, are caused by germs. This came to be known as the germ theory of disease.

Considered the father of microbiology, Louis Pasteur demonstrated that many diseases are caused by germs.

in the 1890s, when scientists found that unseen infectious agents could transfer illnesses from sick plants and animals to healthy plants and animals. Over the next forty years, researchers learned that viruses are microscopic organisms, smaller than bacteria, that are equally adept at causing disease.

By the early 1900s, measles was one of the most common infectious diseases in the world. To increase understanding of contagious illnesses, public health agencies began to track the courses of epidemics. During the first half of the century, the United States reported about a half-million cases of measles annually, resulting in hundreds of deaths per year. In the spring of 1934, for example, the United States experienced an especially serious measles outbreak. An article in *Time* magazine, published in March 1934, noted, "Last week Washington was having its worst measles epidemic since 1921. In the White House, granddaughter [of President Franklin Roosevelt] Eleanor Dall was almost over her attack but 555 other Washington children were put to bed with runny noses, watery eyes, coughs and fever."[6] During that week, large numbers of measles cases were also reported in Philadelphia, St. Louis, Salt Lake City, San Francisco, Boston, Cincinnati, Omaha, Memphis, Atlanta, and Little Rock. Moreover, during the drought-ridden 1930s, the state of Kansas alone had forty thousand measles cases and 145 deaths.

Between 1953 and 1963, America's northern neighbor, Canada, reported about eight hundred thousand cases of measles per year, with an average annual death rate of 270. Even remote regions of the world were not spared. During a 1952 measles outbreak among the Eskimo of Ungava Bay, in northern Quebec, almost the entire population fell ill, and 7 percent died. And in 1954 a measles outbreak in Brazil's isolated Xingu National Park wiped out about a tenth of the native population.

Because measles was so dangerous, especially to children, public health officials were anxious to find a way to prevent outbreaks. By the mid-1900s, vaccines were already available for cholera, rabies, smallpox, typhoid, and plague, and scientists strove to develop one for measles. The measles virus was discovered and isolated in Boston, Massachusetts, in 1954 by two virologists, Dr.

John F. Enders and Dr. Thomas C. Peebles. It would be another nine years, however, before Enders and Peebles developed an effective measles vaccine. And it was not until 1969 that another medical research team worked out a vaccine for rubella, another viral disease commonly mistaken for measles.

Rubella Is Named

The measles virus is a member of the genus *Morbillivirus*, in the family Paramyxoviridae, and the rubella virus belongs to the genus *Rubivirinae*, in the family Togaviridae. Thus, though measles and rubella both cause skin rashes, they are not closely related illnesses.

The first description of rubella was made in 1619 by German physician Daniel Sennert, who called the disease "Röteln," which means red rash in German. It was thought to be a type of measles or scarlet fever, or a combination of the two diseases. Thus, rubella was also called scarlatina morbillosa (measles-like scarlet fever), rubeola scarlatinosa (scarlet fever–like measles), hybrid measles, and three-day measles. Sometimes, rubella was termed third disease because it was usually the third rash disease (after measles and scarlet fever) that afflicted youngsters during childhood.

Röteln was often mistaken for other rash-causing illnesses until 1814, when another German physician, Dr. George de Maton, documented "scarlatina" as a separate illness, different from measles, scarlet fever, and other known diseases. Half a century later, in 1866, an English Royal Artillery surgeon, Dr. Henry Veale, named the mild rash-causing disease rubella, a name derived from the Latin word for "little red." In 1881 rubella was finally recognized as a distinct disease by the International Congress of Medicine in London.

Rubella was also commonly called German measles. The origin of this term is uncertain. Some historians think the name is related to the fact that German physicians first described the disease. Other experts suggest the term comes from the fact that the sickness was thought to be "germane to," or related to, measles.

Unlike measles, the early spread of rubella was not closely traced by historians. This was probably due to two factors. First,

Virologist John Enders (pictured on the cover of Time *magazine) and Thomas Peebles developed a vaccine for measles in 1963.*

rubella was confused with other rash diseases, and second, when rubella was identified as a unique illness, it was thought to be relatively harmless until it was linked to birth defects. Alluding to the public's lack of knowledge about rubella, a 1945 article in *Time* magazine observed, "German measles (rubella), as most adults know it, is a pipsqueak disease which produces only a rash and a mild fever. But if pregnant women catch it, it can give

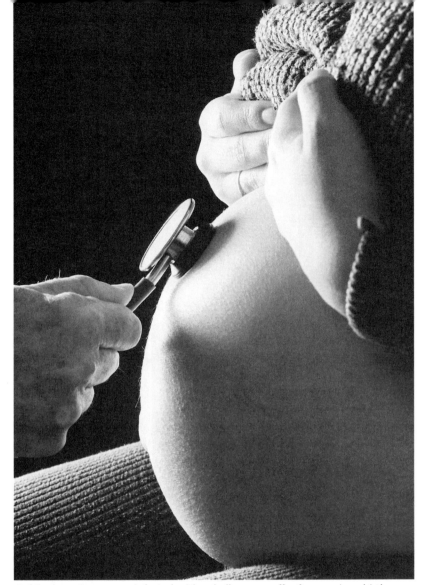

Babies born to women infected with rubella may suffer from serious birth defects, including blindness and mental retardation.

their unborn babies heart disease, cataracts, bad teeth or even make them deaf mutes or idiots."[7]

The Rubella Virus Is Linked to Birth Defects

Scientists believe that the ancestors of the rubella virus were probably insect-borne plant viruses. In fact, other germs in the Togaviridae family, to which rubella belongs, are transmitted from victim to victim by insects. For example, human to-gaviruses that cause dengue fever (a flu-like illness) and yellow fever (a potentially deadly tropical disease) are transferred from one person to another by mosquitoes. The rubella virus is unique because it is the only togavirus that is passed directly from one person to another.

As happened with measles, people who recuperated from rubella became immune to the disease. Therefore, most adults in affected regions eventually became resistant, and the illness became largely (though not totally) a childhood affliction. Rubella is relatively harmless in young children. When rubella strikes pregnant women, however, it can badly damage the developing fetus. This was discovered in 1941 by Dr. Norman McAlister Gregg, the senior ophthalmic surgeon (eye specialist) at the Royal Alexandra Hospital for Children in Sydney, Australia.

In 1940, shortly after the start of World War II, many Australians moved from rural areas to cities and army camps to assist the war effort. A rubella epidemic swept through these congested areas, striking large numbers of children and adults. Soon afterward, in 1941, Gregg noted that many infants in Australia were being born with cataracts (opaque areas in the eyes). After making inquiries, Gregg discovered that the mothers of these babies had contracted rubella while they were pregnant.

In a 1941 report titled *Congenital Cataract Following German Measles in the Mother,* Gregg described newborns with cataracts as being small and difficult to feed, as well as suffering from heart problems. Gregg correctly presumed that the rubella virus had affected fetal development and that infection in the early months of pregnancy caused the worst damage. Later these rubella-related health problems came to be known as congenital rubella syndrome (CRS).

About two decades after Gregg's discovery, a rubella epidemic struck Europe in 1962 and 1963, and the United States in 1964 and 1965. The U.S. outbreak resulted in about 1.8 million cases of rubella, 11,250 miscarriages, 2,100 newborn deaths, and 20,000 children born with CRS. Of the infants with CRS, about 12,000 were hearing impaired, 3,580 were blind, and 1,800 were mentally retarded.

Decline of Measles and Rubella

In many parts of the world, vaccination has helped control measles and rubella. For example, these diseases are no longer endemic (naturally present) in the United States, and the few reported cases of measles, rubella, and CRS in the nation generally occur among immigrants and travelers. Measles and rubella have also sharply declined in Canada, Latin America, Australia, and most nations in Europe over the past ten years. Measles and rubella remain a serious threat in developing nations, however, especially in parts of Asia and Africa. Thus, additional efforts such as expanded disease surveillance and increased levels of vaccination are needed to control measles and rubella in those regions.

Chapter 2

Measles: A Childhood Illness

MEASLES IS A highly contagious viral disease that usually occurs in childhood. The illness, characterized by a skin rash,
fever, runny nose, cough, and red eyes, usually comes on rapidly
and lasts a short time. Complications, however, are common and
can be deadly.

In the era before measles vaccine was developed, measles was
considered just a normal part of life. In fact parents in developed
countries often sent their children to "measles parties" to catch
the disease from youngsters who were already infected. In this
manner, parents hoped to dispense with the disease before their
children reached adulthood. Measles viruses are spread from
person to person by way of respiratory secretions. When a
measles sufferer coughs, sneezes, speaks, or exhales, measles
viruses are spewed into the air. The measles germs, which are
highly contagious, generally infect more than 75 percent of susceptible people who breathe them in. When an unprotected person inhales measles viruses, an incubation period (the length of
time until the first symptoms appear) follows. This can range
from 7 to 14 days, but generally lasts 10 to 11 days. During this
phase, the measles viruses multiply and disperse through the
victim's body.

Like all viruses, measles microbes must enter living cells to re-
produce. Upon infecting a susceptible person, measles viruses
first invade the inner lining of the respiratory system and nearby
lymph nodes. The viruses multiply for two to three days and
then enter the bloodstream and spread. For a short time, measles

viruses are able to evade the body's defenses by hiding in the cells of the reticuloendothelial system. This is an extensive system composed of phagocytes (white blood cells) that normally ingest microbes, worn-out cells, abnormal cells, and foreign substances in the bloodstream.

The measles viruses proliferate in the reticuloendothelial system for several days and then enter the bloodstream and spread once again. The second dispersion usually starts 5 to 7 days after the initial infection and lasts for about 4 to 7 days. During this period, the viruses infect the skin, conjunctiva (the membrane covering the surface of the eye), respiratory system, urinary system, gastrointestinal system, central nervous system, and other organs—where they keep multiplying. At this point, 7 to 14 days after the initial infection, the first symptoms of measles appear.

Course of the Disease

The earliest signs of a developing disease, which emerge immediately after the incubation period, are called the prodrome. For measles, the prodrome consists of the three Cs—cough, coryza (runny nose), and conjunctivitis (red eyes and tearing caused by inflammation of the conjunctiva). Fever, achiness, headache, swollen glands, and photophobia (sensitivity of the eyes to light) are also common during this period. The fever rises during the course of the illness and may reach 103°F to 105°F (39.4°C to 40.6°C).

A day or two after the prodrome, Koplik spots emerge on the inner surface of the patient's mouth, near the back molars. These spots, which are characteristic of measles, are named after Henry Koplik, an American pediatrician who first described them in 1896. The Koplik spots are bright red with bluish-white centers, about 0.04 to 0.12 inches (1 to 3mm) in diameter. Twenty-four to forty-eight hours after the Koplik spots appear, on the fourth or fifth day after the prodrome, the spots start to fade and the typical measles rash begins to develop.

The distinctive measles rash, called a morbilliform rash, is a maculopapular rash. The name derives from the fact that the rash is composed of macules (flat spots) and papules (raised spots),

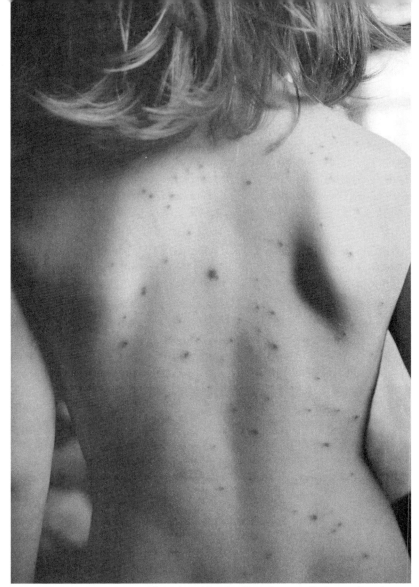

The measles rash is caused by white blood cells trying to eliminate the virus from blood vessels.

0.04 to 0.39 inches (1 to 10mm) in diameter. The rash, which usually does not itch, is caused by white blood cells that gather to destroy measles viruses in the small blood vessels. The measles rash starts on the forehead and behind the ears, and then spreads downward to the neck, torso, limbs, palms, and soles of the feet. This dispersion takes about twenty-four to thirty-six hours. The papules are generally separate but may merge, especially on the upper body. The rash, which is deep red, becomes darkest on the seventh or eighth day after the prodrome.

Once the spots appear, measles patients may become extremely ill. During a measles epidemic in Ireland in 1999, for example, more than one hundred children had to be hospitalized and eight needed intensive care because of their symptoms. Speaking of the severity of the illness in some youngsters, Professor Donald Gill, a senior pediatrician at Temple Street Children's Hospital in Dublin, observed, "[The children] have a very florid rash that covers their body. They are extremely miserable; they just lie down; they want to be left alone; they want to sleep. They won't eat. . . . They run high fevers. Many of them have had a really severe cough, and developed pneumonia."[8]

In most cases, the immune system of the measles victim mounts a strong defense against the disease. The immune system, which consists of a network of white blood cells, proteins, tissues, and organs, works in unison to fight invading microbes. The white blood cells are the main weapons of the immune system. They are produced and stored in the spleen, bone marrow, thymus gland, and lymph nodes, and constitute two basic groups: phagocytes, which engulf and digest invading organisms, and lymphocytes, which identify foreign microbes and produce antibodies to destroy them. Antibodies are assisted by a group of proteins called complement, which help kill bacteria, viruses, and infected body cells. Thus, a few days after the morbilliform rash is fully developed, on the ninth to eleventh day after the prodrome, the papules start to disappear. They fade in the same order they appeared, first from the head and neck, and then from the torso and limbs. During this recovery period, the papules change from red, to purple, to yellow-brown before they fade completely. The average course of measles, from the prodrome until the rash starts to disappear, is usually about ten days.

The measles victim sheds viruses from the mouth and nose, and can transmit the disease from just before the prodromal symptoms appear to about four days after the morbilliform rash develops. These symptoms help doctors to diagnose the disease.

Diagnosing Measles

Physicians may suspect measles in patients who exhibit a cough, runny nose, conjunctivitis, and photophobia. A definite diagnosis of measles is usually made when Koplik spots appear. Since measles is rare in the United States and many other industrialized countries, a laboratory confirmation of the illness may be desired. Several procedures can be used to demonstrate

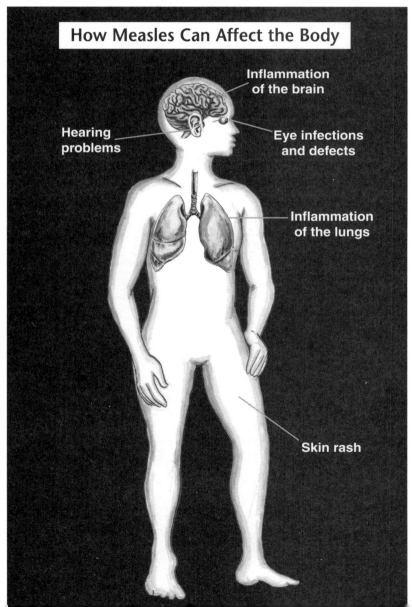

How Measles Can Affect the Body

Inflammation of the brain

Hearing problems

Eye infections and defects

Inflammation of the lungs

Skin rash

the presence of measles viruses in a patient. One scientific technique uses samples taken from a sick person's throat or urine. If measles viruses are present in the samples, the microbes will grow in laboratory tissue cultures, where lab technicians can identify them. In a second procedure, a sample of a patient's blood serum is tested for measles antibodies, which are produced by the body to fight off germs. The presence of the antibodies confirms the presence of measles viruses. A third method, used in Great Britain, employs a radioimmunoassay technique to test for measles antibodies in a sample of a victim's mouth fluids. In this procedure, a radioactive substance is attached to measles antibodies so they can be recognized and measured. In a fourth technique, samples from a patient's throat or urine are stained with immunofluorescent dyes, which give off light. When the dyes attach to measles antibodies, the antibodies can be identified and quantified by the light they give off. A positive result with any of these procedures confirms a diagnosis of measles. Patients diagnosed with measles, however, sometimes exhibit unusual symptoms.

Unusual Types of Measles

Unusual measles symptoms may arise in individuals who received certain kinds of vaccines or medications before being infected with the disease, or in people who have defective immune systems. One aberrant reaction to measles infection is called atypical measles syndrome (AMS). First identified in the middle of the twentieth century, AMS is generally seen in patients who were vaccinated with ineffective or improperly refrigerated measles vaccines. For example, some measles vaccines produced in the mid-1960s did not work correctly. People who received these ineffectual vaccines were, and still are, not protected against the disease, and, in fact, are more sensitive. Experts suggest this may be due to a decrease in hemagglutination-inhibition antibodies. These antibodies, when present, inhibit measles viruses from attaching to and infecting cells. Because of immune system damage, people with AMS exhibit unusually severe symptoms when they contract measles.

AMS begins suddenly with a high fever, a cough, a headache, muscle pain, and abdominal discomfort. The measles rash may appear one to two days later and frequently surfaces first on the wrists or ankles. The rash is customarily made up of macules and papules, but it may consist of tiny red spots. Unlike a normal measles rash, parts of the AMS rash may be itchy, or composed of blood-filled or fluid-filled blisters. Thus, AMS is sometimes mistaken for other diseases such as scarlet fever, chicken pox, or Rocky Mountain spotted fever. In addition to unusual measles symptoms, AMS patients may also suffer from temporary hepatitis (inflammation of the liver), pleural effusions (fluid in the cavity around the lungs), swelling of the hands and feet, and pneumonia. The pneumonia may persist for more than three months, and in severe cases the damaged lungs may take several years to recover completely. Atypical measles syndrome can be prevented by revaccinating susceptible people (who had been improperly vaccinated) with an effective measles vaccine before they catch the disease.

Another unusual reaction to measles infection is called modified measles. This is a mild sickness contracted by people who are partially resistant to the disease. Three groups of patients may exhibit modified measles: newborn babies who still have some of the antibodies received from their mothers in the womb; people who were vaccinated against measles but are still slightly susceptible; and people who, soon after being exposed to measles viruses, received immune globulin (a medicine containing antibodies) to lessen the severity of the illness. Modified measles is usually distinguished by an extended incubation period, a mild prodrome, and a sparse rash that disappears quickly. By contrast, a third aberrant type of measles infection, called hemorrhagic measles, is quite severe.

Hemorrhagic measles, also called black measles, is generally seen in people who are immunosuppressed (that is, they have lowered resistance to disease because of reduced numbers of circulating white blood cells). Several types of immunosuppressed people may be susceptible to black measles: people who have a congenital (inborn) inability to fight infection; people suffering from leukemia or lymphoma (cancers involving white blood

Folk Remedies for Measles

Before the advent of modern medicine, folk remedies were commonly used to treat illnesses. For measles, folk medicines were prescribed to prevent the disease, or if people were already infected, to bring out the rash and cure the patient.

According to folklore, measles could be averted by wearing one of the following remedies around the neck: a tobacco bag filled with burned corn meal, or a bag filled with asafetida (an unpleasant-smelling herb). For people who already had measles, folk wisdom dictated that the spots must be brought out to rid the body of disease-causing substances. To bring out the rash, a patient might be given a hot bath, wrapped in warm blankets, and given a medicinal potion. Rash-inducing "teas" could be made from any of the following substances: rabbit feces, goat feces, sheep feces, sage leaves, elder blossoms, red clover blossoms, sassafras, or corn shucks. After the measles rash developed, ointment was often dabbed on the spots to reduce the patient's discomfort. Some popular folk salves were made from turmeric powder, lime, and water; vinegar and cornstarch; and Epsom salts and water.

cells); patients who are receiving radiation therapy or chemotherapy for cancer; patients with illnesses, such as HIV/AIDS, that depress the immune system; and people receiving high-dose or long-term treatment with corticosteroid drugs to reduce the symptoms of inflammation. Corticosteroids are generally prescribed to treat chronic conditions like asthma, allergies, and juvenile arthritis. However, a side effect of corticosteroids is suppression of the immune system.

Because many immunosuppressed patients have reduced numbers of white blood cells, they may not develop a typical measles rash. Thus, hemorrhagic measles is commonly characterized by very high fever, 105°F to 106°F (40.6°C to 41°C); bleeding from the mouth, nose, and intestinal tract; difficulty breathing; seizures; and delirium (mental confusion). Moreover, patients with black measles often develop severe complications and generally remain contagious for several weeks longer than the average measles sufferer. In some cases, complications of hemorrhagic measles result in death. People with normal measles may also experience complications, but they are usually less severe. Medical treatment can often help measles victims, especially those with more common forms of the illness.

Treatment for Measles

Health agencies recommend that parents contact a doctor immediately if they suspect their child has measles. If the doctor confirms that the illness is measles, he or she will notify health bureaus that keep track of measles outbreaks and will direct the parents to watch for and report complications, such as ear infections or pneumonia. Parents are also counseled to keep track of the child's temperature and to notify a physician if it rises above 103°F (39.4°C). Basic treatment for measles includes reducing pain and fever with acetaminophen, drinking large amounts of clear fluids, gargling with salt water to relieve sore throat, employing a cool-mist vaporizer to reduce coughing and ease breathing, eating healthy foods, and resting the eyes. The eyes of a measles patient may be very sensitive to light and have an irritating discharge. If this is the case, doctors advise caregivers to gently wipe the eyes with a clean, wet cloth and to keep the patient's room dim. The American Academy of Pediatrics also recommends vitamin A supplements for seriously ill measles patients between six months and two years old. Taking these supplements helps people to avoid serious complications, such as blindness, that may result from infection with measles. Pointing out the benefits of vitamin A, an article from Allina Hospitals and Clinics notes that "vitamin A deficiencies . . . cause [measles] to be more severe, even fatal. Vitamin A supplements reduce the severity and complications of measles in children. Vitamin A also reduces the risk of death in infants with this disease."[9]

If measles patients develop secondary bacterial infections like ear infections or bacterial pneumonia, physicians usually prescribe antibiotics. These medicines, which kill bacteria, are not effective against the measles virus itself. Doctors may prescribe antiviral medicines such as acyclovir, used to treat herpes virus infections, or ribavirin, used to treat respiratory syncytial virus infections. Acyclovir and ribavirin, however, are not always effective against the *Morbillivirus* that causes measles. Thus, in most cases components of the patient's immune system, including white blood cells, antibodies, and interferon (chemicals that prevent viral replication), are left to combat the disease on their own.

Advances in medical treatment have reduced the global impact of measles, and vaccination has lowered the frequency of epidemics. Nevertheless, measles outbreaks continue to occur.

Measles Outbreaks Continue

Measles epidemics are especially common in war-torn and poor nations, which often have low vaccination rates. The exact number of measles cases in these regions is not known because infectious diseases are underreported due to incomplete surveillance and limited medical facilities. However, some medical assessments indicate that the majority of measles cases in the early twenty-first century occurred in Asia and Africa. In 2002, for example, there were 14,492 reported measles cases in Indonesia, 10,241 in Thailand, and 51,780 in India. In 2003 a single city in the Philippines reported hundreds of measles cases and at least eleven deaths. Additional Asian nations that reported large numbers of measles cases in the early 2000s include Vietnam, Afghanistan, Cambodia, Myanmar, Laos, and others.

The risk of a measles epidemic in Southeast Asia was heightened by dreadful natural disasters in 2004 and 2005. On December 26, 2004, a massive earthquake hit northern Sumatra, Indonesia. This spawned tsunamis (tidal waves) that killed and injured hundreds of thousands of people in countries around the

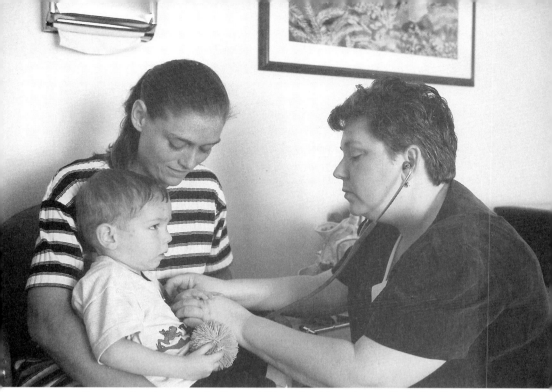

To prevent serious complications, children should receive medical attention at the first sign of a measles infection.

Indian Ocean, including India, Sri Lanka, Malaysia, Maldives, Indonesia, and Thailand. Aftershocks of the earthquake in the following months contributed to the death toll and damage. International health officials noted that destruction of health facilities, water systems, and sanitation systems in Southeast Asia, along with overcrowded conditions in shelters for displaced persons, put millions of people at risk of diseases like measles, influenza, malaria, cholera, typhoid fever, hepatitis, and others. According to medical experts, measles may kill 30 to 40 percent of children left in unsanitized situations like this. Thus, emergency medical workers hurried in to vaccinate people against the disease. Limited numbers of health-care workers, however, and chaos in the region made it impossible to vaccinate everyone. Therefore, sporadic outbreaks of measles occurred across the areas affected by the earthquakes and tsunamis.

In the early 2000s, Africa reported even more incidences of measles than Asia. In 2001, for instance, the total number of reported measles cases in sub-Saharan Africa, including Burundi,

Secondary Infections Associated with Measles

Secondary infections occur when a person is already sick with another illness. In many cases, secondary infections are able to take hold because the patient's immune system is busy fighting the original disease. Among the most common secondary infections associated with measles are pneumonia and ear infections.

Ear infections usually arise in the middle ear, located inside the head behind the eardrum. The middle ear is connected to the throat by a tiny canal, called the eustachian tube, which allows air to move in and out of the middle ear. A respiratory infection, like measles or a cold, can block the eustachian tube. This allows trapped bacteria to grow in the middle ear. When white blood cells congregate to attack the germs, the middle ear fills with pus and swells. As a result, the patient experiences pain, fever, and hearing problems. If the infection is severe, the eardrum may rupture. In most cases, doctors prescribe antibiotics to treat ear infections.

Bacterial pneumonia is another secondary infection that is often associated with measles. Bacterial pneumonia occurs when a microbe grows in the air sacs of the lungs. The resulting immune response causes the air sacs to fill with fluid, making the lungs less able to take in oxygen and expel carbon dioxide. The symptoms of bacterial pneumonia may include fever, chills, chest pains, shortness of breath, fatigue, abdominal pain, and a cough with bloody or yellow phlegm. Physicians usually prescribe antibiotics to clear up bacterial pneumonia, which can be life threatening if left untreated.

Kenya, Nigeria, Senegal, South Africa, and Zimbabwe, was 492,116. In December 2003 the Central African Republic reported about 150 cases of measles with at least thirty-seven deaths. Additional African countries that reported numerous cases of measles in the early 2000s include Angola, Ethiopia, Democratic Republic of the Congo, Rwanda, Sudan, Zambia, and others. Referring to measles fatalities among African children, a 2005 article from the United Nations Children's Fund (UNICEF) observes, "The measles death toll in Africa is so high—every minute one child dies—that many mothers don't give children real names until they have survived the disease."[10]

Because measles continues to plague Asia and Africa, international health agencies are especially anxious to increase control measures in those regions. Thus, the Measles Initiative was launched in 2001 as a partnership between the American Red Cross, the United Nations Foundation, the World Health Organization (WHO), the Centers for Disease Control and Prevention (CDC), and UNICEF. The Measles Initiative plans to vaccinate

In 2004 members of UNICEF meet with people in the Darfur region of Sudan as part of a program to immunize 2.6 million children against measles.

200 million African children in the early twenty-first century with the goal of drastically reducing measles-related death rates on that continent. Moreover, the Measles Initiative, the International Federation of the Red Cross, the Red Crescent Societies,

Measles outbreaks are virtually unknown in industrialized nations, such as the United States, where vaccination rates are extremely high.

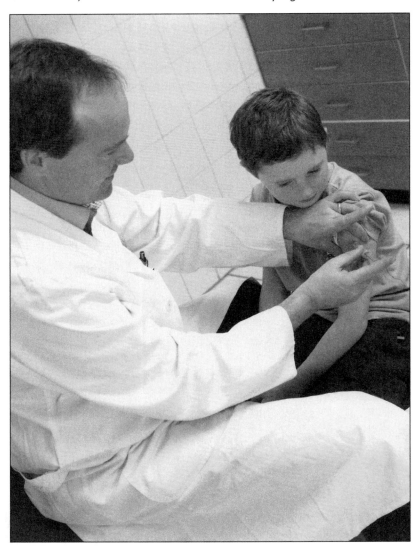

the Global Alliance for Vaccines and Immunization (GAVI), the Bill and Melinda Gates Foundation, and the governments of Australia, Canada, Japan, and the United Kingdom are committed to undertaking a worldwide measles control program.

Measles in Developed Nations

In contrast to developing regions, measles outbreaks are rare in industrialized countries, like the United States, which commonly have high vaccination rates. For example, a 1999 report from the CDC states that the measles virus is no longer endemic to the United States. However, extensive international travel makes it easy for people to carry diseases from undeveloped to industrialized parts of the world. Thus, even developed nations are not immune to measles outbreaks.

Measles outbreaks in developed countries are usually seen among unvaccinated immigrants from Asia and Africa and among citizens who refuse to be vaccinated for religious or other personal reasons. In February 2001, for example, an American couple adopted a ten-month-old baby from China and brought the child home. Upon arrival in Texas, the child fell ill and was diagnosed with measles. An investigation by the CDC and other health agencies soon identified fourteen associated measles cases in seven states: New York, Ohio, Illinois, Indiana, Minnesota, Missouri, and Texas. The victims included ten children who were recently adopted from China, two adoptive mothers, a sibling of an adopted child, and a caretaker. A similar incident occurred in January 2004, when a nine-month-old boy from Alabama contracted measles during a trip to the Philippines. Upon his return, the child infected ten other children in his day-care center and two adults.

Sometimes, American adults carry measles into the country. In March 2004, for instance, an American college student from Iowa, who had been exempted from receiving a measles vaccination for nonmedical reasons, returned from a trip to India. On his way home, the young man passed through the Detroit Metro Airport on his way to Cedar Rapids, Iowa. Soon after arriving in Iowa, the student was diagnosed with measles. Because the student had passed through Detroit, the Michigan Department of Community Health rapidly issued press releases and contacted people who had been in the student's vicinity in order to warn people of their possible exposure to measles. Local health authorities also informed hospitals and physicians to step up surveillance for measles, and medical centers quickly organized measles vaccination clinics. This helped prevent a measles outbreak in the region.

Due to such strict surveillance, measles is quite rare in the United States, and from 2001 through 2003 only 216 measles cases were reported. The majority of victims were international visitors to the United States and U.S. residents exposed to measles while traveling overseas. Most other developed nations also reported relatively small numbers of measles cases in the early years of the twenty-first century. This varied from country to country, however. Australia, for instance, had about 50 incidences of measles in 2003. By contrast, Europe reported 10,500 cases of measles in 2002. Some nations, like Greece, Norway, and Portugal, reported fewer than 10 incidences of measles, while Italy and Germany each reported about 5,000 cases. The relatively large numbers of measles cases in Italy and Germany were attributed to immigrants as well as to native residents who refused to be vaccinated. Clearly, measles continues to cause problems for human populations. Thus, scientists and health-care workers persist in their efforts to control this and other childhood diseases.

Chapter 3

Rubella: A Mild Rash with Potentially Serious Consequences

RUBELLA IS A mild, highly contagious viral disease that usually strikes during childhood. Prior to the development of rubella vaccine, the disease periodically struck populated regions all over the world. Records indicate that small outbreaks occurred every year, and major epidemics broke out every six to nine years. In temperate climates, rubella epidemics were most common in late winter and early spring, but the disease was present throughout the year.

The illness is characterized by a rash, swollen glands, and low fever, and like measles, usually comes on quickly and lasts for a short time. Unlike measles, rubella was considered a relatively harmless illness until the mid-1900s, when it was discovered to cause birth defects in the babies of infected women. Afterward, parents in developed regions began sending their children to "rubella parties" with infected youngsters. This was meant to ensure that they developed immunity to rubella as youngsters, before the disease could have serious consequences. Even boys were exposed to rubella, so they would not contract the disease as young men and pass it on to susceptible women.

Rubella most commonly strikes youngsters between three and ten years old, though it can afflict people of all ages. Like measles,

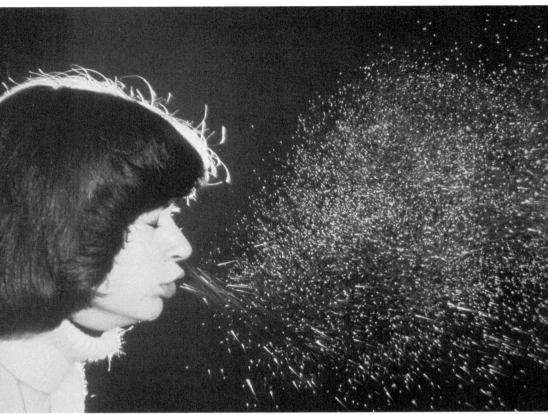

The measles and rubella viruses can be spread through the air when an infected person coughs or sneezes near someone else.

the rubella virus is spread from person to person by way of respiratory droplets. When a rubella victim speaks, coughs, sneezes, or exhales, rubella viruses are expelled into the air. An unprotected person contracts rubella by inhaling these viruses. This can happen during casual contact with an infected person or by encountering viruses that have been released into a car, room, or other confined space. Rubella is not as contagious as measles, but it spreads fairly easily among unprotected persons.

When inhaled, the rubella viruses first infect the cells of the nasopharynx (top of the throat), upper respiratory tract, and local lymph nodes. There, they multiply rapidly. After about five to seven days, the viruses enter the bloodstream and spread throughout the body. The viruses invade additional tissues and continue to multiply for about one to two weeks. The incubation period for rubella ranges from 12 to 23 days, but it usually lasts from 16 to 18 days. During this period, the rubella viruses multiply and disperse through the victim's body, after which the symptoms of rubella begin to appear.

Course of the Disease

Some youngsters infected with rubella have a slight fever for twenty-four hours before the telltale rash appears, and some children demonstrate no prodrome (early symptoms) before the rash emerges. Moreover, rubella can be so mild, particularly in young children, that no rash or other obvious symptoms appear at all. Thus, the illness goes undetected in about 30 to 50 percent of cases.

Rubella is generally more serious in older children, teens, and adults, all of whom usually exhibit a one- to five-day prodrome before the rash develops. Prodromal symptoms may include a fever of 99°F to 101°F (37.2°C to 38.3°C), a sore throat, a stuffy or runny nose, a headache, conjunctivitis, shivering, loss of appetite, fatigue, and swollen glands behind the ears and neck. Swollen glands, in fact, may begin a week before the rash appears and remain for several weeks.

The rubella rash starts on the face and quickly spreads down to the torso, and then to the limbs, and lastly to the hands and feet. It is usually a macular (flat) rash, composed of small, reddish-pink spots that do not itch. Though similar to the measles rash, the rubella rash is less extensive and fades more quickly. Victims of rubella may also exhibit small red dots, called Forschheimer spots, on the soft palate inside the mouth. The exact cause of the rubella rash is uncertain, but like the measles rash, it may result from the assault of the patient's immune system on the virus.

Additional symptoms that may accompany rubella infection in adults are arthritis and arthralgia (inflamed, swollen, painful joints). These symptoms occur in about 60 percent of infected women but are rare in men. Any joint can be affected, but inflammation usually occurs in the fingers, wrists, knees, and ankles. The pain and swelling usually clear up in three or four days, but severe inflammations may take a few weeks to heal. In

Rashes

In addition to measles and rubella, childhood diseases that trigger rashes include chicken pox, roseola, hand-foot-and-mouth disease, and fifth disease. Chicken pox is caused by the varicella-zoster virus. Afflicted youngsters develop hundreds of itchy, fluid-filled blisters that burst and scab after a few days. The blisters, which appear in successive groups, start on the scalp, face, chest, and back, and spread from there. Roseola, caused by human herpesvirus 6, generally affects infants and toddlers. Victims break out in a rose-colored rash that appears on the chest, back, limbs, neck, and face. Hand-foot-and-mouth disease is caused by coxsackie virus A16. Sick youngsters develop mouth sores and a rash composed of very small, painful blisters on the hands and feet. Fifth disease is caused by human parvovirus B19. Affected children first de-

rare instances, the joint difficulties can continue or return over several years. In men, additional symptoms of rubella may include testalgia and orchitis (inflammation and pain in the genitals). These symptoms generally recede when the patient recuperates. Another condition seen occasionally, in about one out of three thousand rubella patients, is thrombocytopenia (a decrease in blood platelets needed for blood clotting). This disorder may cause nosebleeds; bleeding into the kidneys, brain, and gastrointestinal tract; and bleeding into the skin, resulting in small, purple spots just under the outer skin layer. These symptoms may last from days to months, but most patients recover as their immune system combats the disease.

Soon after rubella viruses infect a patient, the victim's immune system produces white blood cells and antibodies that destroy

velop a bright red rash on the cheeks, giving the appearance of slapped cheeks. About a day later, a rash with a lacy appearance appears on the child's arms and legs.

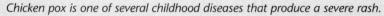

Chicken pox is one of several childhood diseases that produce a severe rash.

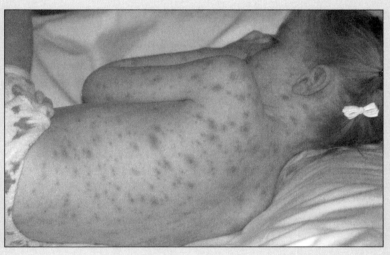

the microbes. Consequently, the rubella rash and other symptoms usually start to disappear in three to five days. The rash fades in the same order it appeared, first from the head, then from the torso, then from the limbs, and finally from the hands and feet. The rubella patient is most contagious while the rash is erupting; however, the rubella sufferer expels viruses, and therefore, can transmit the disease from about seven days before the rash emerges to around five to seven days after the rash appears. Rubella, therefore, may sometimes be spread by victims who show no outward signs of the disease. In fact, infants with CRS (infants infected with rubella before birth who may suffer from deafness, cataracts, and other symptoms), generally exhibit no rash or other overt signs of rubella. Nevertheless, the babies may be contagious for about a year after birth. During that time, the children can infect unprotected people in their vicinity, including caregivers and infants in day-care centers. To protect unvaccinated people, physicians commonly suggest that children or adults diagnosed with rubella remain isolated from others during the infectious phase of the disease.

Diagnosing Rubella and CRS

Diagnosing rubella by symptoms alone is difficult because similar rashes are seen in other diseases like measles, scarlet fever, and roseola. Therefore, physicians usually confirm a diagnosis of rubella using laboratory tests. In one laboratory technique, samples are taken from the suspected rubella victim's throat, blood, or urine. If rubella viruses are present in the samples, the germs

Special care must be taken to isolate infected people from day-care centers and schools, where diseases such as measles are easily spread among children.

will grow in laboratory tissue cultures, where they can be identified by lab workers. This procedure is expensive and not used for routine diagnoses of rubella.

In more commonly used diagnostic procedures, laboratory technicians test samples of a person's blood serum for rubella antibodies. A positive test for antibodies confirms the presence of rubella viruses (either now or in the past) in the patient's body. This procedure is sometimes performed on women of childbearing age to find out whether they had rubella in the past and are therefore resistant to the illness. Several methods can be used to recognize rubella antibodies.

One technique used to identify rubella antibodies in blood serum is called a hemagglutination-inhibition (HAI) assay. In this test, rubella antibodies, if present, inhibit blood clotting in solutions containing chicken blood cells. A second blood serum test for rubella is called an enzyme-linked immunosorbent assay (ELISA). In this test, rubella antibodies, if present, become stained green. Several other laboratory tests for rubella, such as indirect immunofluorescence tests, use immunofluorescent dyes. These dyes, which give off light, attach to rubella antibodies in the samples. Hence, when rubella antibodies are present, they can be identified and measured.

Antibodies can also be used to diagnose infants with CRS. At birth, the blood of a child with CRS contains rubella antibodies, some derived from the mother and some produced by the infant. The antibodies start to break down soon after birth, however, and can rarely be detected by the time the child is eighteen months old. Rubella viruses can also be found in babies with CRS, in the nasopharynx, throat, urine, blood, and cerebrospinal fluid. Like rubella antibodies, the viruses start to dwindle shortly after birth and generally disappear by the time the child is one year old. Thus, physicians commonly conduct antibody and viral tests early if they suspect that a child is afflicted with CRS.

CRS is sometimes difficult to diagnose because infected newborns may appear normal. In a 1997 interview for an Australian program called *The Health Report*, Patrick Ellis explained the delay in diagnosing his daughter Mandy:

She was seven weeks old before we found there was anything wrong with her. She was a good, well-behaved baby, never cried, never made a fuss. Of course she didn't, because she didn't hear anything [because she was deaf]. Nothing was waking her up. Then I came home one day from work [and] the wife had obviously been crying . . . and she said, 'There's something wrong with the baby's eye . . . the pupils of the eye are grey.' So we subsequently took [Mandy] to the doctors and he said 'Yes,' [she has CRS] and it sort of snowballed from there.[11]

Early physical signs and symptoms seen in children afflicted with CRS may include low birth weight, less than 5.5 pounds (2.49kg), feeding problems, digestive system abnormalities, and diarrhea. Common eye defects in youngsters with CRS are cataracts (cloudy areas in the lenses of the eyes), microphthalmia (abnormally small eyes), nystagmus (rapid back-and-forth movement of the eyeballs), squint (inability to focus on an object with both eyes), and abnormal pigment changes in the retina (the light-sensitive layer that lines the back of the eyeball). Other symptoms of CRS may include pneumonia, congenital heart disease, hepatosplenomegaly (enlargement of the liver and spleen), jaundice (a yellow discoloration of the skin and whites of the eyes), microcephaly (an abnormally small head and brain), meningoencephalitis (inflammation of the brain and surrounding membranes), anemia (reduced number of red blood cells), and temporary blood abnormalities that result in a thrombocytopenic rash (purplish or reddish-brown rash), and a tendency to bleed easily. Additional abnormalities associated with CRS, such as developmental delay, mental retardation, and hearing impairment, usually become obvious during the first few months of life. In fact, one of the most common clinical signs of CRS is damaged hearing, as the daughter of Patrick Ellis reveals.

If hearing tests and other symptoms indicate that a child has CRS, health-care workers in many countries are required to submit a report to the appropriate health agency. A standard report includes the following information: where and when the baby was born, the baby's signs and symptoms, results of the baby's

Live virus cells are needed to manufacture the measles and rubella vaccines. Here, a technician works with living cells under sterile conditions in a virus laboratory.

laboratory tests, a history of the mother's immunizations, a history of the mother's rash illnesses during pregnancy, and a history of the mother's travel during pregnancy. This information can help health agencies track outbreaks of rubella and CRS. The ultimate goal is to reduce the number of children afflicted with CRS. Infants born with CRS who exhibit serious symptoms, such as hearing impairment, vision damage, and other disabling conditions, can sometimes be assisted with appropriate medication and therapy. Medical treatment may also benefit children and adults suffering from rubella.

Treatment for and Recovery from Rubella

As with measles and most other viral infections, no specific treatment exists for patients with rubella. The symptoms are usually

How Rubella Affects Newborns

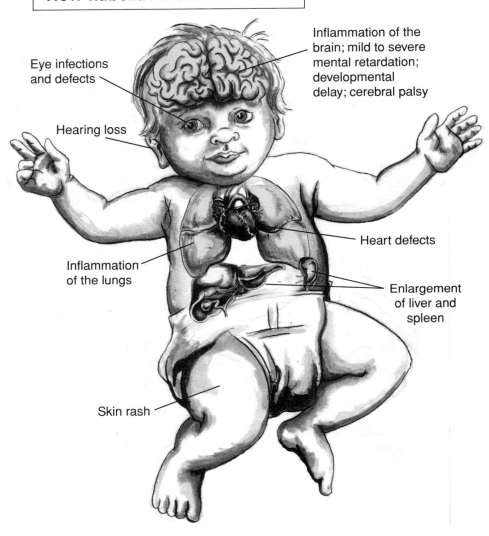

Eye infections and defects

Inflammation of the brain; mild to severe mental retardation; developmental delay; cerebral palsy

Hearing loss

Heart defects

Inflammation of the lungs

Enlargement of liver and spleen

Skin rash

so mild, however, that no medication is needed, and doctors are often content to let the disease run its course. Sometimes children infected with rubella experience discomfort from fever and aches. In this case, physicians generally recommend bed rest and acetaminophen or ibuprofen. Health professionals warn against giving children aspirin to relieve discomfort. Research has shown that children who take aspirin during or after viral illnesses, like rubella, measles, and others, are in danger of developing Reye's syndrome. This illness, most commonly seen in children and teenagers, is caused by an abnormal accumulation of salicylate (an ingredient in aspirin) in the liver, brain, and other organs. Reye's syndrome is generally marked by symptoms such as vomiting, dry heaves, fatigue, confusion, restlessness, aggression, anxiety, and irrational behavior. In very serious cases, victims may experience convulsions and delirium, sometimes resulting in coma (deep and prolonged unconsciousness) and even death.

Adults afflicted with rubella are more likely to suffer from discomfort and pain than children. Again doctors commonly recommend acetaminophen or other over-the-counter medicines to alleviate the discomfort. If adults experience more serious rubella symptoms, like arthritis or testalgia, they may require anti-inflammatory drugs or other medications.

Sometimes patients recuperate from rubella but still experience unusual sequelae (a condition that follows after having a disease). For example, an uncommon reaction that has been linked to rubella is a drastic increase in weight, caused by disruption of the endocrine system (ductless glands that regulate body functions). This apparently happened to the "world's heaviest twins," Billy and Benny McGuire, who were professional wrestlers in the 1970s and 1980s. During a 2004 interview for "The Home of Pro Wrestling's Legends Web site," Benny McGuire talked about their weight gain as a result of having rubella. "We didn't start gaining weight until we [were] about four years old," observed Benny. "We had the German measles and that messed up our pituitary tract. They took us to Baptist Hospital and Duke University. They put us on a thousand calorie per day diet . . . and we still gained weight. [German measles] got our system upset. We didn't burn the calories that we took in."[12] Viral damage to the pituitary gland, or "master gland" of the endocrine system, can cause it to lose control of the thyroid gland, which helps govern weight. Thus, by the age of sixteen, each of the twins weighed six hundred pounds. Such a drastic increase in weight is considered serious because medical researchers have found that obese people sometimes develop illnesses such as heart disease and high blood pressure that shorten their life spans.

Rubella rarely has a serious outcome like this either in children or adults. Moreover, the majority of people who recover from rubella become immune to the illness and cannot become infected again. On rare occasions, however, individuals do contract

Hypothyroidism

Children born with CRS sometimes develop chronic conditions such as thyroid gland dysfunction when they become teenagers or young adults. The thyroid gland is a small gland in the neck, just below the Adam's apple, or larynx. The function of the thyroid gland is to produce two thyroid hormones, thyroxine (T4) and triiodothyronine (T3). These hormones are released into the bloodstream and carried to all the tissues and organs, where they control metabolism, the chemical processes in the body that regulate weight.

When the thyroid gland malfunctions, it can become underactive, causing hypothyroidism, or overactive, causing hyperthyroidism. Thyroid dysfunction in CRS victims is usually hypothyroidism, a condition characterized by inadequate amounts of T3 and T4. This can cause a variety of symptoms, such as depression, irritability, difficulty concentrating, memory loss, weakness, fatigue, sensitivity to cold, and, in women, heavy menstruation. Other common signs of hypothyroidism are constipation, muscle aches, dry skin, hair loss, hoarse voice, swollen eyes, dry hair, and weight gain. Most patients with underactive thyroid glands demonstrate a combination of several of these symptoms. If the condition becomes severe, there may be a decrease in heart rate, a drop in body temperature, and heart failure. Eventually, severe hypothyroidism, if left untreated, may lead to a life-threatening coma.

A rare side effect of rubella is drastic weight gain. Identical twins and professional wrestlers Billy and Benny McGuire blamed their extreme size on childhood rubella.

rubella for a second time. In these cases, the second bout is extremely mild with few or no symptoms. If a pregnant woman becomes reinfected with rubella, the woman's immune system quickly destroys the viruses. Thus, physicians believe there is little danger to the fetus. However, unusual cases have been reported in which infants with CRS were born to mothers who were reinfected with rubella during pregnancy. Because rubella can be very dangerous to pregnant women, medical authorities are anxious to control outbreaks of the ailment.

Rubella Outbreaks

Although more than half of all nations now use a rubella vaccine, the disease still breaks out in undeveloped parts of the world and among unvaccinated populations elsewhere. For example, Romania experienced a countrywide rubella epidemic in 2003 that resulted in about 115,000 cases of the disease, mostly among school-aged children. Similarly, in 2002 and 2003, the South Pacific islands of

Tokelau, Tonga, and Samoa reported about 20,000 cases of rubella. The South Pacific epidemic resulted in the deaths of three children from complications of the disease. A rubella outbreak also occurred in Madrid, Spain, in 2003, mostly among immigrant women who had been born in Ecuador, Colombia, the Dominican Republic, and Argentina, where vaccination is not always available. Nineteen rubella victims were identified, fourteen of them women of childbearing age. None of the patients had been vaccinated against rubella. A more serious rubella epidemic broke out among unvaccinated children and adults in Japan, beginning in November 2003. By mid-2004, the number of reported rubella victims reached almost 2,000.

A rubella outbreak also occurred in the Netherlands, starting in fall 2004 and extending to winter 2005. At least 128 confirmed cases of rubella were reported, largely among children who be-

In 1998 and 1999, outbreaks of rubella in New England and the Midwest were traced to Central and South American immigrants working in American meat-packing plants.

longed to the Dutch Orthodox Church. Most of the Netherlands patients had not been vaccinated against rubella for religious reasons. Kamchatka and Kazakhstan, both members of the former Soviet Union, also had rubella outbreaks in the early 2000s. Two villages in Kamchatka, in eastern Russia, reported about 75 cases of rubella in 2004. The outbreak was believed to stem from a sick child who attended summer camp in the affected region. The Kamchatka villages were placed under quarantine until the local populations could be vaccinated. During that same year, a much more extensive rubella epidemic occurred in Kazakhstan, a large country south of Russia. In that year, Kazakhstan had 15,104 reported cases of rubella, but health experts believe the number may have been even higher.

By contrast, in the 1990s the United States averaged only 232 reported cases of rubella per year. Most U.S. victims were young adult Hispanic immigrants from nations where rubella vaccination is not routine. In December 1998, for instance, over 80 suspected cases of rubella broke out in neighboring cities of New York and Connecticut, and in September 1999, 116 cases of rubella were reported in Nebraska, Iowa, and Minnesota. The majority of the U.S. victims were immigrants from Central and South America who worked in (or whose relatives worked in) meat-packing plants. A similar phenomenon has been seen in Great Britain. Most recorded cases of rubella since 1999 have occurred in people who emigrated from Africa, Asia, or Greece.

By 2005 rubella was no longer a major public health risk in most of North America. In March of that year, public health administrators in the United States and Canada announced that rubella had been virtually eliminated from those countries. Speaking of this landmark event, Dr. Julie Gerberding, director of the CDC, states, "This is a major milestone in the path toward eliminating rubella in other parts of the world, including the Western Hemisphere and other regions that have committed to this very, very important health goal."[13] North American officials noted that the few cases of rubella within their borders in 2004, nine in the United States and seven in Canada, had been travel-related. Rubella vaccination is also curbing the disease in other parts of the Americas. In 2003 Dr. Carlos Castillo Solórzano of the Pan American Health Organization (PAHO) announced that rubella vaccination programs had greatly reduced the incidence of the disease in Latin America, from 135,000 reported cases in 1998 to 923 cases in 2003. Moreover, in November 2004 PAHO set the goal of eliminating rubella from the Americas by 2010. Talking about the possibility of ridding the world of rubella, Dr. Steve Cochi, acting director of the CDC's National Immunization Program, notes, "Global eradication [of rubella] is possible, but given other medical priorities, it's not on the front burner. Right now, the world needs to focus its resources on completing polio eradication [polio is a viral disease that can cause paralysis, permanent disability, and death] and the initiative to reduce measles deaths."[14]

Because rubella cases in developed nations are often travel-related, health agencies keep track of rubella outbreaks in different countries and on cruise ships. Health authorities note that cruise ships can be especially dangerous because infectious diseases, like rubella, influenza, stomach virus, and others, are easily spread when numerous people are housed in a confined space. Moreover, some of the passengers and crew aboard cruise ships may come from countries that have low vaccination rates for rubella and other diseases.

Several U.S. cruise lines experienced rubella outbreaks in the late 1990s and early 2000s. For example, in April, May, and June 1997, a cruise ship that regularly sailed between Florida and the Bahamas reported a total of seven cases of rubella among the ship's staff. A survey indicated that 95 percent of the crew had not been born in the United States and that most of the staff had not been vaccinated against rubella. Similarly, in July 1997 another U.S. cruise ship that traveled between Florida and the Bahamas reported sixteen cases of rubella among its crew members. Again, most of the crew was foreign-born and unvaccinated against rubella. Several years later, in August 2002, a Disney cruise line staff member came down with rubella during a voyage. Because of occurrences like these, the CDC recommends that all women of childbearing age who plan to travel on cruise ships make sure they are vaccinated against rubella.

Outbreaks of rubella on cruise ships have been attributed to low vaccination rates in the home countries of some crew members, as well as the confined space on board.

Rubella epidemics are alarming because they may result in infants born with CRS. Health authorities are anxious to curtail these devastating consequences of the disease, and have devised strategies to improve rubella prevention and control around the world. These plans include promoting efforts to expand rubella vaccination levels, especially among women of childbearing age; instituting prompt and vigorous control measures whenever rubella outbreaks are reported; and increasing surveillance of rubella and CRS so methods can be developed to prevent rubella infection in women who may become pregnant. Widespread implementation of such measures could greatly reduce the number of children born with CRS.

Chapter 4

Dire Effects of Measles and Rubella

MOST PATIENTS RECOVER from measles with no lasting ill effects. Thus, many people think of measles as a disease that is not especially harmful. However, measles can be a grievous, even fatal, illness. Similarly, rubella is generally thought of as a mild disease. Nevertheless, rubella can also have dire consequences. Among the most common harmful effects of diseases are complications, or additional medical problems, caused by the illness. In the case of measles, about 30 percent of patients experience one or more complications during or after the normal course of the disease.

Measles Complications

Complications of measles are most common in children under five years old, and adults twenty years old and over. Some complications result from measles viruses invading white blood cells, especially monocytes (circulating white blood cells) and phagocytes. White blood cells normally help the body fight off germs, so measles sufferers may experience temporary immunosuppression if too many white blood cells are infected. This makes these sufferers more susceptible to secondary infections like ear infections (seen in about 1 out of 10 patients), viral or bacterial pneumonia (seen in about 1 out of 20 patients), and encephalitis (seen in about 1 out of 1,000 patients).

Signs of encephalitis, or inflammation of the brain, may be a severe headache, a stiff neck, convulsions, extreme drowsiness, difficulty waking up, or loss of consciousness. Encephalitis can be especially dangerous, since the brain swelling associated with the disease may lead to blindness, deafness, convulsions, coma, or even death. Describing the consequences of encephalitis in a young measles victim, Dr. Kenneth Moss, a pediatrician who treated patients at Cincinnati Children's and General Hospital in the 1960s, writes:

> One day I was on the neurological ward at the Children's Hospital and saw a very handsome lad of about ten years old. He was sitting in a large crib and rocking back and forth, staring vacantly, and moaning. When I reviewed his chart, it revealed that he'd suffered the measles complication of encephalitis. . . . For this boy it meant he was left in a nonverbal, blind state from damage to his nervous system from the measles virus.[15]

Even patients who recover from measles encephalitis may continue to experience various long-term problems such as recurrent seizures or mental retardation.

Other secondary conditions that may accompany measles include croup (a respiratory disease characterized by a barking cough), laryngitis (inflammation of the larynx), bronchitis (inflammation of the bronchial tubes), myocarditis (inflammation of the walls of the heart), hepatitis (inflammation of the liver), streptococcus infections, and thrombocytopenia. Measles can also reactivate and aggravate tuberculosis, a very serious disease that damages the lungs and other organs. Some measles victims may also suffer from mouth sores, malnutrition, vomiting and diarrhea (seen in many infants and young children), and vitamin A deficiency. Since the eyes need vitamin A to function properly, blindness may result. Though complications of measles may be serious in any patient, they are particularly dangerous for pregnant women. Side effects of measles may cause an expectant mother to lose the fetus, deliver the baby prematurely, or have a low-birth-weight infant. Very severe complications may even result in the mother's death.

In pregnant women and other patients, secondary effects of measles, if they develop, usually occur during the acute phase of the illness, when the patient has a fever and a rash. Sometimes, however, complications are observed long after a patient appears to have recovered. This may happen when some of the measles viruses evade the patient's immune system and remain in the brain. In time, this causes subacute sclerosing panencephalitis (SSPE), a chronic (long-term or recurring) brain disease causing convulsions, poor muscle coordination, and mental retardation.

One serious complication of measles is encephalitis, which can lead to blindness, as in the case of this girl in Addis Ababa, Ethiopia.

SSPE is a rare condition that affects about one in eight thousand measles victims. The illness usually shows up about eight to ten years after the original measles infection. SSPE is an extremely severe condition that usually results in the death of the patient. Most other measles complications are less dangerous but may also be fatal on occasion.

Death from Measles

In developed nations, death from measles occurs in about two cases out of one thousand. Death in children is usually due to pneumonia, encephalitis, or dehydration caused by diarrhea. Death in adults generally results from encephalitis. By contrast, fatalities from measles are relatively common in poor countries, where there may be one hundred or more deaths out of one thousand measles cases. This may be due, in part, to poor nutrition. Speaking of the toll of measles on malnourished children, a senior health department pediatrician in Chandigarh, India, observes: "Measles is the highest killer disease of malnourished children. Mortality in malnourished children is about 20 times higher than in well-fed children."[16]

Poorly nourished children may be more susceptible to illness because of vitamin A deficiency. Vitamin A has been linked to proper functioning of the immune system, and a shortage of this compound may make it harder for the body to destroy measles viruses. In fact, research has demonstrated that vitamin A supplements can benefit measles victims. Following his work in Africa in the 1990s, Dr. Alfred Sommer, professor and dean at the Bloomberg School of Public Health at Johns Hopkins University in Maryland, noted that vitamin A supplements had helped measles patients in Tanzania. "Knowing that measles often leads to vitamin A loss," observes Sommer, "we had begun to wonder if Africa's high death rates from measles might also be connected with vitamin A deficiency. To test this [hypothesis], children hospitalized with measles in Tanzania were given vitamin A capsules. The measles death rate fell by half."[17] Due in large part to the work of Sommer and others, WHO now recommends that children in developing nations receive vitamin A supplements.

As a result of a deficiency in Vitamin A, which helps regulate the immune system, malnourished children are highly susceptible to the measles virus.

This is credited with saving the lives, as well as the sight, of hundreds of thousands of children each year. Unlike measles, rubella patients rarely experience long-term ill effects from the disease. On occasion, however, rubella sufferers experience serious complications or other undesirable effects.

Dangerous Consequences of Rubella

Though severe complications are uncommon with rubella, some children and adults experience life-threatening side effects. One serious complication of rubella, estimated to occur in about one out of six thousand cases, is encephalitis. Rubella encephalitis can cause headache, vomiting, stiff neck, drowsiness, convulsions, and nerve damage. Most patients recover from rubella encephalitis, but in some cases death may occur.

In rare instances, a delayed complication of rubella, called rubella panencephalitis, develops eight or more years after the initial infection. This condition causes severe brain damage, including cerebral vasculitis (inflammation of the blood vessels of the brain), loss of neurons (nerve cells), demyelination (loss of protective sheaths around nerve cells), and death of brain tissue. Rubella panencephalitis is generally fatal within three years of the appearance of symptoms. Health experts speculate that rubella panencephalitis may be caused by rubella viruses that remain in the brain of a victim after he or she recuperates from the illness, or by rubella antibodies deposited in the brain's blood vessels during the initial infection.

Some of the gravest consequences of rubella occur when the disease afflicts expectant women. When a pregnant woman contracts rubella, the virus spreads through her body and infects many tissues, including the placenta. The placenta is the tissue that connects the mother's body to the fetus, supplying the fetus with food, water, and oxygen from the mother. Soon after rubella viruses invade the placenta, they can travel to, and infect, the developing baby. This is especially true in early pregnancy. Thus, up to 90 percent of infants born to mothers who contract rubella during the first sixteen weeks of pregnancy develop CRS.

Rubella infection after the sixteenth week of pregnancy does not usually cause serious birth defects. Scientists believe that, by this stage, the fetal immune system, combined with antibodies from the mother, can control the viruses. On occasion, however, rubella infection in later pregnancy can affect the developing infant. For example, rubella-associated heart defects and deafness have been reported after infection as late as twenty-four and twenty-eight weeks of pregnancy, respectively. In addition, some researchers suggest that infection as late as twenty-eight weeks of pregnancy can slow the growth of the fetus. Fetuses younger than four months, however, are in the most danger of developing congenital rubella syndrome.

Development of Congenital Rubella Syndrome

Once rubella viruses enter a young fetus, they remain throughout the pregnancy and for about a year afterward. Doctors believe this happens because the immature immune system of the young fetus cannot destroy the viruses. Scientists suggest that the fetus's developing immune system may be disabled by viral infection of young immune cells, which may be unable to multiply normally. Moreover, though rubella antibodies pass from the mother to the fetus, not enough antibodies get through in early pregnancy to eliminate the germs.

Rubella viruses in the developing fetus are thought to spread by way of the fetal circulatory system. Thus the viruses can disperse into many tissues and organs, causing numerous and severe abnormalities. The defects associated with CRS are thought to be caused by two major factors: prevention of cell division in the fetus, which results in abnormally small tissues and organs; and destruction of fetal cells, which leads to damaged tissues and organs.

When rubella infects the circulatory system of the early fetus, the viruses injure or kill the cells that line many blood vessels. This can lead to blood clots in numerous small vessels, causing the death of tissues and organs throughout the developing infant. Rubella also damages the lining of the heart, leading to cardiac abnormalities. Several types of heart defects are linked to rubella. One cardiac abnormality, called patent ductus arteriosus (PDA) is characterized by an open duct between the pulmonary artery (the artery that carries blood from the heart to the lungs to be oxygenated) and the aorta (the artery that carries blood away from the heart to be distributed to the rest of the body). In fetal circulation, a duct between these arteries allows blood to bypass the lungs, since oxygen is acquired from the mother. After birth, however, the duct is supposed to close to keep blood flowing in the correct direction. In babies with PDA, however, the duct does not seal. This may cause an irregular pulse, a heart murmur (an abnormal sound as blood flows through the heart), and in severe cases, congestive heart failure (a condition in which the weakened heart cannot pump enough blood to body organs). A second kind of heart abnormality, called ventricular septal defect (VSD), is marked by an abnormal opening between the right and left ventricles (lower chambers) of the heart. This defect allows blood to pass directly from one ventricle to the other, which does

A pregnant woman with rubella can infect her unborn child, whose immune system is not sufficiently developed to fight off the virus.

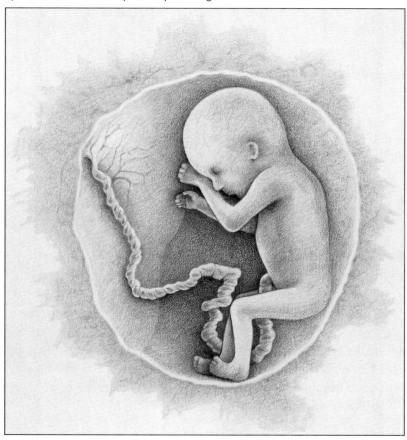

Hearing Tests

Hearing loss occurs in 70 to 90 percent of infants with CRS. Moreover, hearing impairment is the only overt sign of CRS in about half these cases. Though doctors routinely test for hearing problems in suspected CRS victims, detecting hearing loss in babies is difficult. Audiometry (hearing tests) in this age group are unreliable, and distraction testing, in which an infant's head turns toward a new sound, is not always sensitive or accurate.

To alleviate these problems, medical researchers have developed two scientific methods to measure hearing ability in infants: otoacoustic emissions (OAE) and auditory brainstem response (ABR). OAEs are sounds produced by the movement of hairs in the cochlea (the spiral tube in the inner ear) in response to various tones presented to each ear. OAEs originate in the cochlea, but the middle and outer ear must be able to transmit the sounds back to a recording microphone to be measured. Therefore, OAE testing can help experts determine hearing ability as well as the health of the ears. The ABR test works differently. It measures brain-wave activity in the hearing centers of the brain in response to a series of clicks in each ear. To be "heard" by the brain, the clicks must pass through the ear to the auditory nerve, which connects to the brain. Thus medical experts can use the ABR test to determine hearing ability and the condition of the ears. Hearing loss in children with CRS can interfere with the normal development of speech and language, and make socialization difficult.

not happen in normal circulation. Symptoms of VSD in children may include shortness of breath, paleness, failure to gain weight, fast heart rate, sweating while feeding, and frequent respiratory infections. If the hole in the heart is large, the child may eventually develop congestive heart failure. A third heart defect, called pulmonary valve stenosis (PVS), is a condition in which blood flow from the right ventricle of the heart is partially blocked. This inhibits blood flow to the lungs. Rubella infection of the heart and blood vessels may continue throughout fetal development and after birth. If circulatory damage is severe, death may result.

Damage to Eyes and Ears

In addition to heart defects, many infants with CRS exhibit eye abnormalities. For example, infants born with CRS frequently have cataracts, or opaque areas, in the lens of each eye. The lens is normally a clear, rounded structure that focuses light onto the retina. Medical experts speculate that fetal cataracts form when rubella viruses enter the developing lenses after damaging the blood vessels that supply the eyes. Rubella viruses can remain in the eyes for up to three years after birth, causing increasing cloudiness in the lenses.

Rubella viruses may also harm other parts of the eye, including the retina, the iris (the colored portion of the eye), and the ciliary body. The ciliary body is the structure in the eye that secretes the transparent liquid (aqueous humor) in the eyeball. It also contains the ciliary muscle, which changes the shape of the lens when the eye focuses. Over time, rubella infection may lead to other eye problems such as retinopathy (inflammation of the retina), a detached retina (a curtain over the field of vision), and glaucoma (enlarged eyeballs due to increased internal pressure). Overall, rubella viruses can cause grievous damage to a child's eyes, resulting in severely impaired vision or blindness. Jane Mulholland talks about the blindness and other problems suffered by her son Roger, who was born with CRS. "When Roger was born, he was a small baby, covered in blood blisters," observes Mulholland. "Within a day it was confirmed that he was blind and had severe brain damage. He was later found to have four separate heart defects and to be completely deaf. He has endured years of surgery . . . and the whole family is affected by his illness. . . . It doesn't go away for any of us."[18]

Rubella viruses usually injure an infected infant's ears as well, leading to hearing difficulties, as in Roger's case. In fact, the most common problem associated with CRS is sensorineural deafness. This is an irreversible type of hearing loss caused by viral damage to the auditory nerve in the cochlea (spiral tube) of the inner ear. Medical experts suggest that rubella viruses enter the fetus's inner ear by way of the blood supply and damage the cells on the inner and outer walls of the cochlea. Most children with CRS are born with a hearing impairment. Moreover, continuing injury to the inner ear after birth may cause deafness to increase in early childhood. Sometimes, though, the hearing loss may appear later. In 1991 the Helen Keller National Center published the results of an ongoing survey of late-onset manifestations of CRS. In one case, the mother of a twenty-four-year-old man noted that her son's hearing had declined over the preceding five years; in another case, the parents of a twenty-year-old woman reported that their daughter's ability to hear had decreased after she reached adulthood. There have also been instances in which individuals with CRS who had normal hearing in early childhood suddenly developed mild to severe sensorineural hearing loss. The latest age at which this has been reported to occur is ten years old.

Mental Handicaps and Other Physical Impairments

In addition to their other problems, people with CRS may be mentally handicapped because of damage to the central nervous system. Rubella infection of the blood vessels in the fetal head may diminish the oxygen supply to the brain. This can cause mild to severe mental retardation with spastic diplegia, a type of cerebral palsy (muscle disorder) characterized by stiff, jerky movements of the limbs, especially the legs. After the baby is born, rubella viruses remaining in the cerebrospinal fluid (the liquid in the cavities of the brain and in the central canal of the

People with Congenital Rubella Syndrome (CRS) often suffer from damage to the central nervous system, which can lead to permanent mental and physical impairments.

spinal cord) may cause cerebral vasculitis and encephalitis. The encephalitis can last for years, increasing brain damage.

Besides having physical abnormalities, fetuses infected with rubella generally exhibit slow growth. This may be caused by reduced or slower cell division in rubella-infected cells. In one study, the average birth weight of babies with CRS was found to be only about 65 percent of the average birth weight of uninfected infants. Sometimes poor growth and fetal damage kills the fetus, and the mother has a miscarriage or stillbirth. The exact rate of fetal death linked to rubella is not known, however, because CRS can be difficult to detect. Even newborns that survive fetal infection with rubella may have symptoms that are hard to recognize. In a 1978 report, Jeanette Lloyd described how long it took to determine the extent of damage suffered by her daughter, Michelle. "In Michelle's case," wrote Lloyd, "the full extent of damage [from CRS] was only realized after years of tests, confirmed and unconfirmed diagnosis, constant visits to the different physicians involved, and exhausting trial and error decisions due to the lack of capable physicians and correct diagnostic procedures at our disposal."[19]

In some cases, CRS victims develop additional health problems when they become teens or young adults. These difficulties may include progressive spasticity (increasing stiffness in the muscles), ataxia (lack of muscular coordination), mental deterioration, seizures, radiolucent bone disease (loss of bone tissue), hypertension (high blood pressure), and thyroid gland dysfunction. The thyroid gland secretes a hormone called thyroxine, which helps regulate metabolism and weight. Thus, some CRS victims experience an immense weight gain when they reach young adulthood. In the survey conducted by the Helen Keller National Center, the family of a female CRS victim reported that, at the age of sixteen, the girl had experienced an unusual weight gain and developed hirsutism (abnormal hairiness). Another example of late-onset problems associated with CRS is illustrated by Brenda Fredrick, whose mother contracted rubella about two weeks into her pregnancy. Born with CRS in 1959, Brenda grew slowly, was hearing impaired, and lost an eye at age four because of glaucoma. Still, Brenda was able to complete college and begin graduate school. Soon afterward, however, Brenda's illness grew worse, and she had to leave school and enter a rehabilitation center. Brenda's mother, Marilyn Fredrick, describes Brenda's problems:

> In her second year of graduate school, Brenda began to deteriorate both physically and mentally. During this time, she was diagnosed with Hashimoto's thyroiditis [a disease resulting in enlargement of the thyroid gland and decreased production of thyroid hormones], mitral valve prolapse [degeneration of the

valve between the left atrium and left ventricle of the heart, which can lead to heart failure], glaucoma in her remaining eye, cystic disease of the ovaries [an endocrine disorder that causes malfunctioning ovaries, irregular menstruation, excessive hair growth, and obesity], constant urinary tract infections, spastic colon [a condition characterized by abdominal pain and constipation or diarrhea], and additional hearing loss. . . . She also displayed very bizarre behaviors [such as disappearing from the rehabilitation center in the middle of the night].[20]

Brenda's condition continued to deteriorate until she could no longer walk and talk. With intensive medical treatment, Brenda improved enough to move around with a walker and talk a little. Yet she may never be able to completely take care of herself.

Individuals with CRS may also develop insulin-dependent diabetes mellitus as children or adults. This illness is caused by gradual destruction of the pancreas by the rubella virus. The pancreas produces insulin, which regulates the amount of sugar in the blood. People without a healthy pancreas accumulate too much sugar in their blood (a condition known as hyperglycemia), resulting in frequent urination, excessive thirst, extreme tiredness, blurred vision, and other symptoms of diabetes. Another possible late-onset effect of CRS, beginning about eight or more years after birth, is progressive rubella panencephalitis. Late-onset conditions linked to CRS may be caused by several factors: rubella damage during the fetal stage, continuing rubella infection after birth, cell destruction caused by rubella antibodies, and immune system problems linked to rubella infection. Though there is no specific treatment for CRS, some symptoms can be alleviated with medicine and therapy.

Treatment and Prevention of Congenital Rubella Syndrome

Some problems that are common among newborns with CRS, like low birth weight, feeding difficulties, diarrhea, blood anomalies, enlarged liver, and thrombocytopenic rash, usually clear up without treatment. Other conditions, including pneumonia and meningitis, can be treated with medication. More serious complications such as eye or heart defects can sometimes be improved or corrected with early surgery, and children with vision loss or hearing impairment can often benefit from special education programs that provide communication and learning skills. Youngsters with mental retardation may also profit from early special education, as well as physical therapy and occupational therapy. In some cases, however, little can be done to help children with CRS. In a 2003 media release from the Immunisation Advisory Centre in New Zealand, the mother of a child with CRS recalls how disabled her daughter was:

 # Treating Congenital Rubella Syndrome

There is no cure for CRS. Individual symptoms of the condition, however, can often be treated. Heart defects and irregularities of the genital and urinary tracts can often be surgically corrected. Gastrointestinal problems such as trouble swallowing can be treated using therapy or meal programs.

Young people with eye damage may benefit from an operation, glasses, or—if vision is severely impaired—mobility training. And deafness can be improved by speech and language therapy and hearing aids. Other symptoms of CRS, such as hypertension, diabetes, and seizures, can often be treated with medication.

Children with behavior problems may benefit from psychiatric treatment and medicine. Mentally retarded young people and people with cerebral palsy may be assisted by occupational and physical therapy. Occupational therapy helps children perform tasks in their daily lives such as washing,

While I was still in the maternity home they detected cataracts on [my daughter's] eyes, and she had a heart murmur, and they felt that the outlook was very bleak. They didn't think she would survive, and they thought that she would be severely mentally retarded. This was an absolutely devastating experience for me. . . . My daughter now is 33. She does not speak, she has no eyesight at all, she is completely deaf, her sensory input is through vibration and smell. . . . One of the common things she does is the sort of puzzles that you would give to a 2 year old, you know the wooden type puzzles which she does all by touch. . . . It has been very painful for me, and I think, I will carry that for the rest of my life.[21]

dressing, and eating. Physical therapy helps relieve pain and improve flexibility, coordination, balance, and motion. Even with extensive treatment, the abilities of children with CRS may be severely limited.

Although CRS cannot be cured, drugs and therapy can improve a victim's quality of life.

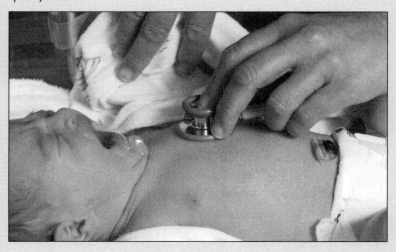

Though CRS damage is not always this extensive, the condition always causes health problems. Thus, medical agencies in many countries collect information about CRS victims.

Public Health Efforts

CRS is uncommon in the United States, which reported only eighty cases from 1998 to 2004. In about half the cases, the mothers of the afflicted children were from developing nations, including Mexico, the Dominican Republic, Honduras, Colombia, and the Philippines. To reduce the frequency of CRS, the March of Dimes has been advocating global programs to control rubella. WHO and UNICEF have assisted in this effort by asking all cooperating countries to submit annual reports detailing incidences of CRS within their borders. The data is not complete because some nations collect little or no information about CRS. However, using available information, health experts estimate that about 110,000 infants are born with CRS every year, mostly in developing countries. To reduce cases of CRS, the March of Dimes has encouraged all nations to initiate rubella vaccination programs. This has had some positive results. For example, in Latin America, CRS is no longer a problem in the eighteen English-speaking Caribbean countries and Uruguay. Also, in the early 2000s, inoculation programs to curb CRS were begun in Kyrgyzstan and Moldova, both members of the former Soviet Union. Other developing countries in the Americas, eastern Europe, and Asia are also expected to institute CRS control programs. Moreover, the European region of WHO hopes that rubella vaccination will reduce CRS cases in that area to less than one per one hundred thousand births by 2010.

Vaccination against diseases like rubella and measles can be very effective in preventing outbreaks. With respect to rubella, the March of Dimes is particularly concerned about females of childbearing age. Therefore, the agency recommends that all women be vaccinated against rubella before they get pregnant. If a susceptible pregnant woman is exposed to rubella, there is no way to prevent the disease. However, doctors may prescribe antibodies called human normal immunoglobulin (HNIG) to help

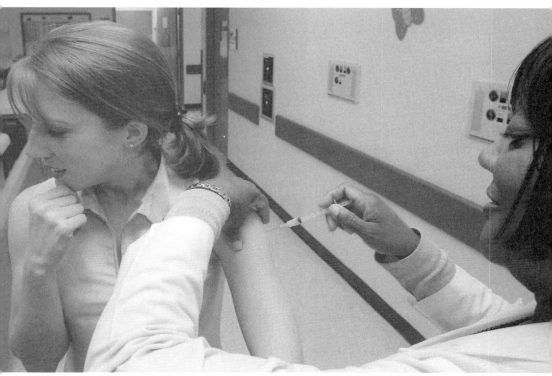

To reduce the frequency of CRS, women should get the measles and rubella vaccines before becoming pregnant.

fight off the infection. The medication may reduce the symptoms of rubella and cut down the spread of rubella viruses through the mother's body. This does not eliminate the possibility of the baby developing CRS, yet evidence suggests that the severity of birth defects associated with CRS may be reduced.

For measles, vaccination has been very effective in controlling the disease. Health experts estimate that measles inoculations have prevented about 80 million cases and 4.5 million deaths annually. Still, because vaccination levels are not uniformly high all over the world, measles continues to cause nearly a million deaths each year. Someday, universal vaccination may eliminate the death and devastation caused by both measles and CRS.

Chapter 5

Development and Use of Measles and Rubella Vaccines

VACCINES CAN HELP prevent contagious diseases and save lives. Before the advent of vaccines, millions of people died from illnesses such as measles, smallpox, bubonic plague, diphtheria, pertussis, yellow fever, tetanus, and influenza. Emphasizing the value of vaccines, Dr. Anthony S. Fauci, director of the National Institute of Allergy and Infectious Diseases, observes, "The impact and importance of vaccines cannot be overstated—these powerful public health tools provide safe, cost effective and efficient means of preventing illness, disability and death from infectious diseases."[22] The United States and many other nations currently have low incidences of most vaccine-preventable diseases. The microbes that cause the illnesses still exist, however, and medical researchers continually strive to develop new and better vaccines to combat them.

A vaccine, such as the ones used against measles or rubella, contains dead or inactivated germs (usually bacteria or viruses) that trick the body into thinking it is being attacked by microbes. The immune system fights off the microbes by producing antibodies that destroy them. The antibodies remain in the body for years and are then available to demolish "real" germs of this type if they are encountered at a future time. Thus, measles vaccine prepares the body to fight off measles viruses, and rubella vaccine primes the body to destroy rubella viruses.

To develop an effective vaccine against a bacteria or virus, knowing the structure of the microbe is helpful. Viruses, such as those that cause measles and rubella, are microscopic organisms composed of two principal parts, a protein envelope and a strand of genetic material. The genetic material, or genome, may be either ribonucleic acid (RNA) or deoxyribonucleic acid (DNA). The two parts of a virus facilitate multiplication. The envelope helps the virus attach to and enter living cells, where the microbe replicates. And the genome contains the instructions for multiplication. Though all viruses are similar is some ways, each specific type has unique characteristics. Thus, the measles and rubella viruses are readily distinguishable from one another.

Measles and Rubella Viruses

The *Morbillivirus* that causes measles is a relatively large microbe, 100 to 300 nanometers in diameter (1 nanometer = 1 millionth of a millimeter). It is pleomorphic (comes in different shapes) but is usually roughly spherical. The measles virus contains six kinds of structural proteins and a strand of RNA. These components are assembled into two basic parts: a central nucleocapsid and an outer envelope. The nucleocapsid is the core of the measles virus. It is a helical structure composed of an RNA strand and three types of proteins: nucleoproteins (N proteins), large proteins (L proteins), and phosphoproteins (P proteins). The nucleocapsid proteins help the genome maintain its shape and assist the genome in directing viral replication.

The outer envelope of the measles virus, which surrounds the nucleocapsid, is composed of lipids (fats) and three additional kinds of proteins: fusion proteins (F proteins), hemagglutinin proteins (H proteins), and matrix proteins (M proteins). The envelope proteins help the microbe attach to and penetrate host cells and assist in the assembly of new viruses. Once a measles virus infects a human cell, replication takes about twenty-four hours. After this, new measles viruses erupt from the cell surface.

The measles virus is genetically stable, so there is only one strain. This differs from some disease viruses, such as flu viruses, which have many varieties (Hong Kong flu, Asian flu, Russian flu, swine flu, and so on). Because there is one strain of measles virus, a single measles vaccine can provide long-term, universal protection anywhere in the world.

The measles virus is rapidly inactivated by acids, ether (an organic solvent), trypsin (a chemical that digests proteins), heat, and light. Thus, the measles virus can only survive in the air or on surfaces for less than two hours. Like the measles virus, the rubella virus is sensitive to heat and light. The rubella virus is also sensitive to organic solvents and detergents, which dissolve the viral envelope. In addition, the infectivity of the rubella virus is reduced after exposure to radiation.

The *Rubivirinae* microbe that causes rubella is smaller than the measles virus and less complex. It is generally round or egg-shaped and has a diameter of about sixty to seventy nanometers. The rubella virus contains three types of structural proteins and a strand of RNA. As in the measles virus, these components are

This electron photograph provides a highly magnified image of the Morbillivirus, which causes measles.

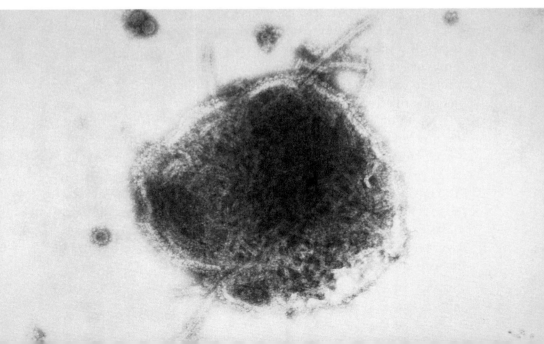

assembled into two basic parts: a central nucleocapsid and an outer envelope. The nucleocapsid, in the center of the rubella virus, is icosahedral (has twenty sides) and appears to have a rounded shape. It is composed of a single strand of RNA and capsid proteins (C proteins).

The outer envelope of the rubella virus, which surrounds the nucleocapsid, is composed of lipids and two additional kinds of proteins. These are called envelope glycoprotein 1 (E1) and envelope glycoprotein 2 (E2). Glycoproteins are proteins with chains of sugars attached. The E1 and E2 glycoproteins join together to form surface projections, or spikes, that cover the envelope of the rubella virus. Once a rubella virus enters a human cell, replication takes about thirty-six to forty-eight hours. After this, the rubella virus multiplies and emerges from the cell surface.

Like the measles virus, the rubella virus is genetically stable and has one primary strain. Therefore, a single rubella vaccine can furnish long-term protection for most individuals.

A Succession of Measles Vaccines

The first person who tried to develop a measles vaccine was Francis Home, the Scottish physician who first proved that measles was contagious. In 1758 Home inserted the blood of measles victims into cuts intentionally made on healthy individuals. Home claimed that this technique, adapted from an inoculation procedure used for smallpox, would cause a mild form of measles. This was supposed to protect people from severe cases of the disease. However, Home's "vaccination" procedure, called morbillisation, was dangerous because it could unknowingly transmit other microbial diseases such as hepatitis, syphilis, and tuberculosis from one person to another. Moreover, morbillisation was not proven to protect people from measles. Thus, it was soon discontinued.

About two hundred years later, in 1954, the American scientists John F. Enders and Thomas C. Peebles, who discovered the measles virus, developed a way to grow it in tissue culture. This finally made it possible to formulate effective measles vaccines. There are two principal kinds of vaccines. One kind, called an inactivated

Viral Replication

Viruses multiply by entering a host cell and taking over the cell's reproductive machinery. There are five main stages involved in this process: attachment, penetration, synthesis, assembly, and release.

During the attachment phase, the virus binds to a specific receptor on the cell membrane of the host cell. Cells lacking the appropriate receptors are not susceptible to the virus.

The virus penetrates the cell in one of several ways. Some viruses pass directly across the cell membrane. Others fuse with the cell membrane and pass their contents into the cell. And some viruses become enclosed in a vesicle, made of a segment of cell membrane that indents and pinches off. The virus is then released from the vesicle into the cell. In all cases, once the virus is inside the host cell it frees its nucleic acid (DNA or RNA), which directs synthesis of new viruses.

During synthesis, the host cell's reproductive equipment produces viral enzymes and components, which then assemble into new viruses. A single infected host cell may produce ten thousand to fifty thousand viruses.

Viral release occurs next. In some cases, the infected cell lyses, or disintegrates, to release the new viruses. In other cases, new viruses bud off the surface of the cell. And in some instances, viruses pass directly from one cell to another by cell-to-cell contact.

vaccine, contains killed microbes. The second type, called a live-attenuated vaccine, contains live germs that have been attenuated (weakened), so they cannot cause serious illness. It took nearly a decade for Enders, Peebles, and their colleagues to attenuate the measles virus, develop a vaccine, perform clinical trials, and have the vaccine licensed and released. Their vaccine, licensed in 1963, was a formalin-inactivated vaccine, prepared by killing Edmonston-type measles viruses (originally derived from a measles patient, David Edmonston) with a disinfectant solution. The vaccine proved unsatisfactory, however, because the killed viruses evoked only a weak immune response that induced only short-term immunity to measles. In addition, there was a danger of vaccine recipients suffering from atypical measles syndrome if they contracted the disease at a later time. Therefore, use of the formalin-attenuated vaccine was discontinued in 1967.

Another measles vaccine, called the live-attenuated Edmonston B vaccine, was also licensed for use in the United States in

Dr. John Enders (pictured), who discovered the measles virus with Thomas Peebles, won the Nobel Prize for the discovery in 1954.

1963. The vaccine was developed by Enders and his coworkers by growing the Edmonston strain of measles viruses in a series of different tissue cultures at 95°F to 97°F (35°C to 36.1°C). The Edmonston viruses were subjected to twenty-four passages (growth cycles) in human kidney cells and twenty-eight passages in human amnion cells (cells derived from the sac that surrounds a human fetus). They were then grown in chick embryo cells (cells derived from chicken fetuses). The purpose of these procedures was to adapt the viruses to grow in chicken cells at low temperatures (compared to human temperature, which is 98.6°F or 37°C). Afterward, the Edmonston viruses were unable to grow well in human cells and could cause little or no harm to people. Nevertheless, they were still able to induce immunity to measles.

The Edmonston B vaccine was immunogenic (that is, it provoked an immune response in the body) and protected people from measles. However, it could cause significant side effects, such as fever, rash, stuffy or runny nose, sore throat, cough, headache, and sometimes convulsions. The side effects could be reduced if a gamma globulin, such as measles immune globulin (MIG), was given with the vaccine. MIG is a mixture of proteins, normally found in the blood, that contains antibodies. Edmonston B vaccine was used from 1963 to 1975. At that time, medical authorities decided its adverse effects were too frequent and severe, and the vaccine was taken off the market.

During the 1960s scientists prepared a number of additional live-attenuated measles vaccines from the Edmonston strain of measles viruses. The Schwarz vaccine, released in the United States in 1965, was obtained by subjecting the Edmonston B viruses to eighty-five additional passages in chick embryo cells at 90°F (32.2°C). The Schwarz vaccine was considered the first measles vaccine to have a sufficiently small risk of side effects. The vaccine was administered to people in the United States for several years. However, it was eventually replaced by a better measles vaccine, the Moraten vaccine (sometimes called the Enders-Edmonston vaccine). The Moraten vaccine was first licensed in the United States in 1968. It is similar to the Schwarz vaccine but contains viruses that were passed through chick embryo cells for an additional forty growth cycles at 90°F (32.2°C). The Moraten vaccine provides excellent immunity to measles and has relatively few side effects. Because of its safety and effectiveness, it is the only measles vaccine now used in the United States.

The Moraten vaccine protects more than 95 percent of vaccinated people against measles. In addition, immunity to measles lasts for at least twenty years, and many medical experts believe its protection is probably lifelong. Moreover, measles inoculations are protective if they are given before or up to three days after exposure to the disease. The measles vaccine is considered safe because, though it contains live viruses, it cannot cause measles in the inoculated person. Moreover, the vaccinated person cannot infect other people with measles. Like the Moraten measles vaccine, the rubella vaccines used now are also considered safe and effective.

Development of Rubella Vaccines

The first three rubella vaccines were licensed for use in the United States in 1969. The original vaccine was developed by Dr. Paul D. Parkman and Dr. Harry M. Meyer at the U.S. National Institutes of Health. This vaccine was produced by passing rubella viruses through African green monkey kidney cells for seventy-seven growth cycles, and then passing them through duck embryo cells (cells derived from duck fetuses). The resulting live-attenuated vaccine was called HVP77 DE-5 (DE for duck embryo). A second live-attenuated rubella vaccine was created by passing rubella viruses through dog kidney cells. This vaccine was called HPV77 DK-12 (DK for dog kidney). A third rubella vaccine was based on the Cendehill strain of rubella viruses, which were grown in rabbit kidney cells. All of these rubella vaccines were administered to people in the United States and provided effective protection against the disease. The dog kidney vaccine was soon removed from the market, however, because of frequent side effects, such as joint pain.

In the 1970s another live-attenuated rubella vaccine was developed by Dr. Stanley A. Plotkin at the Wistar Institute in Philadelphia, Pennsylvania. Plotkin created the RA27/3 rubella vaccine by passing rubella viruses through human diploid fibroblast cells

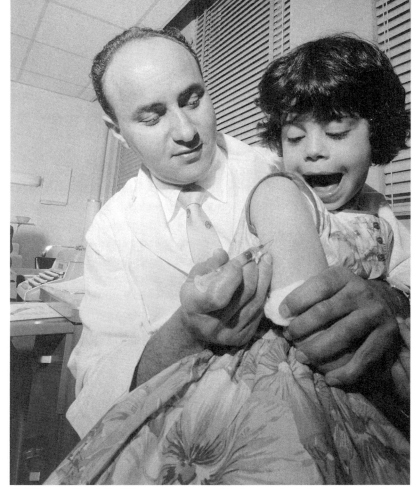

Children in the United States are required to be vaccinated against measles, mumps, and rubella before entering the school system.

(connective tissue cells) for twenty-five to thirty growth cycles. The RA27/3 vaccine, named Meruvax II, was licenced for use in the United States in 1979. Meruvax II had better immunogenicity and fewer side effects than other rubella vaccines, and soon replaced them. It is now used all over the world.

The rubella vaccine is very effective, protecting more than 95 percent of vaccinated people against the disease. Studies have shown that protection endures for at least two decades and is probably lifelong in most recipients. However, a small number of inoculated people do not produce antibodies after one rubella vaccination and require a second inoculation. The rubella vaccine does not cause rubella in inoculated recipients, and vaccinated people cannot infect other people with rubella. For convenience, rubella vaccine is generally combined with measles vaccine to make inoculation simpler and easier.

Handling and Administration of MMR Vaccine

Measles vaccine and rubella vaccine are available in several forms: as individual vaccines, in a measles-rubella combination vaccine, and most commonly in a measles-mumps-rubella combination vaccine, called MMR. In the United States, the MMR vaccine is used almost exclusively. In fact, the Advisory Committee on Immunization Practices (ACIP) recommends that the MMR vaccine be used when protection against any of the individual diseases (measles, rubella, or mumps) is warranted.

The MMR vaccine is given by injection under the skin, usually in the thigh or upper arm. In the United States and other industrialized nations, people generally receive two doses of MMR vaccine: the first at 12 to 15 months of age, and the second at 3 to 6 years of age. In the United States, all fifty states require children to have a second dose of MMR vaccine before they can start either kindergarten, first grade, or another grade as determined by state laws. The second dose of MMR is needed to induce immunity in people who do not have an adequate response to the first injection. Research shows that almost all people who do not react to the first dose of MMR will respond to the second dose. If for some reason a youngster does not get a second MMR inoculation when he or she is between 3 and 6 years old, medical experts generally recommend a "catch-up" vaccination at about 11 to 12 years of age, when the child gets a preadolescent checkup.

Vaccination schedules in developing regions such as parts of Africa, Asia, and Latin America differ from those in industrialized countries. For example, health officials recommend that children in undeveloped nations receive three MMR vaccinations: the first at 6 to 9 months old; the second at 15 months old; and the third at about 5 years old. The first inoculation is needed because infants in undeveloped regions lose the antibodies they get from their mothers more quickly, leaving them unprotected against infection. Medical experts believe this occurs, in part, because women in developing countries often have poor health and low antibody levels, and infants in developing nations lose large quantities of antibodies during frequent bouts with diarrheal illnesses and infections. Unfortunately, babies in developing regions sometimes receive no MMR vaccinations. This may be due to insufficient medical facilities, lack of funds, or other reasons. In these situations, girls may be inoculated when they reach adolescence to prevent congenital rubella syndrome in their children. Though inoculation with MMR vaccine is strongly recommended for most people, it is contraindicated (not recommended) for some people.

People Who Should Not Receive MMR Vaccine

A small number of people should not receive MMR vaccine for medical reasons. The vaccine is not recommended for the following people:

- People who have had a severe allergic reaction to a previous dose of MMR vaccine.

The measles, mumps, and rubella (MMR) vaccine has been used successfully on many children, including these Palestinians in the West Bank city of Hebron.

- People who are allergic to eggs, because the vaccine passes through chick embryo cells.
- People who are allergic to substances in the vaccine, such as gelatin or certain antibiotics (particularly neomycin or polymyxin).
- People who are seriously ill, such as influenza patients or victims of other diseases.
- People with untreated tuberculosis. This is a precaution. Medical reports indicate that tuberculosis can be made worse by measles disease. However, there is no evidence that the measles viruses in MMR vaccine have the same effect.
- People who have recently received antibody-containing blood products, such as gamma globulins, whole blood, or red blood cells. The antibodies might disable the viruses in the vaccine.
- People who cannot combat infections because they are severely immunosuppressed. This includes people who are born immunosuppressed; people who are undergoing radiation therapy or chemotherapy for cancer; people who are receiving long-term corticosteroid therapy for inflammatory conditions; and people with HIV/AIDS who have low white blood cell counts.
- Pregnant women or women who plan to get pregnant within three months. This is a precaution. There is no evidence that MMR vaccine can harm the developing fetus.

People who are permitted to receive MMR vaccine generally suffer few or no ill effects from the vaccinations. On occasion, however, MMR inoculations may cause complications.

Side Effects of MMR Vaccine

MMR vaccine is considered very safe; however, like other medications, it sometimes causes side effects. Some relatively mild side effects might include a reaction at the injection site (burning, stinging, itching, redness, tenderness, or a hard lump), a low grade fever, a runny nose, a sore throat, swollen lymph glands, inflammation of the salivary glands, a mild headache, irritability, and mild discomfort. More severe adverse reactions to MMR vaccine may include a skin rash, a high fever, nausea, a low blood platelet count, bruising or purple spots on the skin, swelling and pain in the joints (mostly in women), double vision, a severe or prolonged headache, extreme discomfort or pain, numbness or tingling of the limbs or extremities, stiff neck, vomiting, and confusion. On very rare occasions, less than once in a million MMR doses, an inoculated person might experience dangerous side effects like meningitis, encephalitis, or seizures.

Some individuals have an allergic reaction to MMR vaccine. Symptoms of an allergic reaction might include hives, a rash, swelling of the face, sudden and severe tiredness or weakness, and itching. In extreme cases, individuals may experience anaphylactic shock. This is a serious, life-threatening allergic reaction characterized by low blood pressure, difficulty breathing, and reduction in body functions. Severe allergic reactions, however, are estimated to occur less than once in a million doses. Because MMR vaccine is effective and has only mild side effects in most cases, health agencies have formulated plans to vaccinate people around the globe against measles and rubella.

Global Control of Measles and Rubella

Most industrialized nations inoculate children against measles and rubella. This is not the case, however, in many developing countries. Thus, international health organizations such as WHO, the March of Dimes, the Pan American Health Organization, UNICEF, and GAVI, as well as national medical agencies, have launched campaigns to inoculate the populations of developing nations with MMR vaccine. In Iran in 2003, for instance, about 33 million people between the ages of 5 and 25 were inoculated with MMR vaccine during a 3-week-long vaccination campaign. The operation, which took 6 years to plan, involved 23,000 vaccination sites, 9,000 mobile teams traveling to remote parts of the country, and 120,000 health workers. Refugees from war-torn Afghanistan, which borders Iran on the east, also took advantage of the inoculation program. Kari Egge, the UNICEF representative in Iran, describes the participation of people from

Allergic Reactions to MMR Vaccine

MMR inoculations are not recommended for people who are allergic to certain ingredients in the vaccine, such as gelatin, neomycin (an antibiotic), or egg products. Substances that trigger allergic reactions, called allergens, affect only those people whose immune systems are sensitive to them. Most people are not sensitive to MMR vaccine, and serious allergic reactions are rare, occurring in less than one in a million doses.

The most severe form of allergic reaction is called anaphylactic shock, or anaphylaxis. This is a life-threatening response that occurs rapidly and involves the whole body. For an anaphylactic reaction to occur, the victim must have been exposed to the allergen, such as MMR vaccine, previously. This is called sensitization. Subsequent exposure to the allergen triggers a heightened reaction, termed a hypersensitivity response. Anaphylaxis may cause symptoms such as faintness, rapid heartbeat, stomach cramps, nausea and vomiting, diarrhea, red and itchy eyes, blotchy skin, hives, drowsiness, and confusion. Sometimes, the victim's lips, tongue, and throat swell, making it difficult to breathe. In addition, the victim's blood pressure may drop, resulting in shock (depression of body functions) and loss of consciousness. An anaphylactic reaction may occur within seconds to minutes of exposure to an allergen such as MMR, though symptoms sometimes take up to four hours to appear. Without rapid medical treatment, anaphylactic shock can cause brain damage, kidney failure, and death.

Afghanistan. "What is unique about this program is that the Afghan refugees are really coming for vaccinations," notes Egge. "Lots of Afghan women have been bringing their children. Afghans are taking full advantage of this."[23] Health authorities believe that global vaccination programs like this could control measles and rubella around the world. There is a potential obstacle to this, however. In some regions, parents refuse to have their children inoculated against measles and rubella because they fear that MMR vaccine causes grave illnesses.

Vaccine Safety

In the 1990s concerns arose that MMR vaccine might cause two serious conditions: autism and Crohn's disease. Autism is a developmental disorder of the brain in which parts of the brain are damaged or do not develop correctly. The condition is characterized by an array of symptoms including difficulty understanding and using language, problems socializing and communicating with other people, inability to cope with changes in routine, trouble dealing with variations in a familiar environment, repetitive body movements or behavior patterns, unusual methods of playing with toys or other objects, and uncommon responses to loud noises and bright lights. Crohn's disease is a chronic inflammation of the digestive tract. Symptoms of the illness include diarrhea, severe abdominal pain, abdominal cramping, fever, fatigue, lack of appetite, weight loss, and skin lesions.

Medical officials hope to decrease people's anxiety about MMR inoculations by distributing the findings of health agencies, such as WHO, the CDC, and others, that have affirmed that no conclusive evidence exists to link MMR vaccine with autism or Crohn's disease. In recent years, however, fears about the dangers of MMR vaccine have resulted in a reduced level of MMR inoculation in a number of developed countries, including Great Britain, Ireland, France, Germany, Italy, and Malta. Even nations with high vaccination rates, such as the Netherlands, have sizable minority communities that decline MMR vaccinations. Thus, there have been outbreaks of measles and rubella in some of these regions. In 2001 the WHO released a statement support-

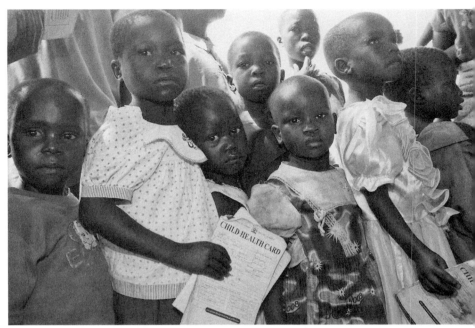

Efforts to eradicate childhood diseases such as measles continue in the Third World. These children are waiting in line for vaccinations in Gulu, Uganda.

ing the use of MMR vaccine. It said, "WHO strongly endorses the use of MMR vaccine on the grounds of its convincing record of safety and efficacy. . . . There has been no new scientific evidence that would suggest impaired safety of MMR. On the contrary, all results from vaccine trials published reaffirm the high safety of MMR vaccine."[24] The April 2003 *Drug and Therapeutics Bulletin,* an independent review from Consumers' Association, also emphasizes the safety of MMR vaccine. It notes,

> Immunization with the combined measles, mumps and rubella (MMR) vaccine gives highly effective protection against all three diseases, and has the potential to eliminate these infections, including congenital rubella syndrome, saving many lives and preventing serious illness. In our view, there is no convincing evidence that MMR vaccine causes, or facilitates development of, either inflammatory bowel disease or autism.[25]

Someday, consistent, universal use of MMR vaccine may eliminate measles and rubella from the world.

Notes

Introduction: Persistent Childhood Diseases

1. Oregon Department of Human Services, "Measles (Rubeola)," 2004. www.dhs.state.or.us/publichealth/acd/measles/index.cfm.
2. Quoted in March of Dimes News Desk, "March of Dimes Supports PAHO Effort to Eliminate Rubella," September 23, 2003. www.marchofdimes.com/printableArticles/9564_9803.asp.

Chapter 1: The History of Measles and Rubella

3. Quoted in UCLA Library, "The UCLA Louise M. Darling Biomedical Library History and Special Collections Division Presents an Online Exhibit: Smallpox," 2000. www.library.ucla.edu/libraries/biomed/smallpox/rhazes.html.
4. Quoted in Robert McCaa, "Spanish and Nahuatl Views on Smallpox and Demographic Catastrophe in the Conquest of Mexico," *Journal of Interdisciplinary History*, March 14, 1994. www.hist.umn.edu/~rmccaa/vircatas/vir6.htm.
5. Quoted in Marie E. Daly, "Disease and Our Ancestors: Mortality in the Eighteenth and Nineteenth Centuries," New England Historic Genealogical Society, 2001–2005. www.newenglandancestors.org/education/articles/NEA/disease_and_our_ancestors_mortality_in_the_eighte_607_1807.asp?print=1.
6. *Time*, "Measles," March 26, 1934. www.time.com/time/archive/preview/0,10987,747256,00.html.
7. *Time*, "German Measles Menace," March 5, 1945. www.time.com/time/archive/preview/0,10987,797155,00.html.

Chapter 2: Measles: A Childhood Illness

8. Quoted in BBC News, "Measles Outbreak Feared," May 30, 2000. http://news.bbc.co.uk/1/hi/health/769381.stm.

9. Allina Hospitals and Clinics, "Vitamin A (Retinol)," April 2002. www.medinformation.com/ac/CAM.nsf/conssupplements/VitaminARetinolcs.html.

10. UNICEF, "Why Are Children Dying?" 2005. www.unicef.org/immunization/index_why.html.

Chapter 3:
Rubella: A Mild Rash with Potentially Serious Consequences

11. Quoted in Australian Broadcasting Company, "The Health Report: Rubella," June 23, 1997. www.abc.net.au/rn/talks/8.30/healthrpt/stories/s69.htm.

12. Quoted in Wrestling Legends.com, "Interview with the Legends: Benny McGuire," 2004. www.1wrestlinglegends.com/columns/interviews/inbm.htm.

13. Quoted in Karen Pallarito, "Rubella No Longer a Threat in the U.S.," HealthDay News, March 21, 2005. www.healthday.com/view.cfm?id=524659.

14. Quoted in Anita Manning, "A Booster Shot Against German Measles," *USA Today*, March 21, 2005. www.usatoday.com/news/health/2005-03-21-german-measles_x.htm.

Chapter 4: Dire Effects of Measles and Rubella

15. Kenneth Moss, "Measles Shots Are Common Sense: Personal Reflections of an Alaska Physician," Immunization Action Coalition, April 26, 2000. www.immunize.org/stories/story29.htm.

16. Quoted in Sourav Sanyal, "Admn Readies to Tackle Measles Cases," *The Times of India*, February 19, 2004. http://timesofindia.indiatimes.com/articleshow/505129.cms.

17. Alfred Sommer, "A Bridge Too Near," in *Nutrition: The Progress of Nations*, United Nations Children's Fund, 1995. www.unicef.org/pon95/nutr0002.html.

18. Quoted in BBC News, "MMR Debate: Mothers' Stories," 2003. http://news.bbc.co.uk/1/hi/health/1113653.stm.

19. Jeanette Lloyd, "Learning About Congenital Rubella Syndrome," *National Parent Network Newsletter*, Winter 1992–1993, pp. 15–17.
20. Marilyn Fredrick, "One Mother's Story of Her Daughter with CRS," Helen Keller National Center for Deaf-Blind Youths and Adults, 1997. www.hknc.org/Rubella_One_Mothers_Story.htm#Return%;20To%20Top.
21. Quoted in Health Professional's On-line Resource Centre, "Rubella Outbreak in the Pacific Islands," Immunisation Advisory Centre, University of Auckland, New Zealand, October 7, 2004. www.immune.org.nz/default.asp?a=625&t=561&View=FullStory&newsID=2.

Chapter 5: Development and Use of Measles and Rubella Vaccines

22. Anthony S. Fauci, "A Commitment to Global Health," National Institute of Allergy and Infectious Diseases, National Institutes of Health, 1999. www.niaid.nih.gov/director/usmed/1999/usmed99text.htm.
23. Quoted in IRIN News.org, "Iran: Mammoth Vaccination Drive Will Benefit 33 Million," December 23, 2003. www.irinnews.org/report.asp?ReportID=38550&SelectRegion=Central-Asia&SelectCountry=IRAN.
24. MMR—The Facts, "Statement on the Use of MMR Vaccine," January 24, 2001. www.mmrthefacts.nhs.uk/library/time line.php?t=showall.
25. *Drug and Therapeutics Bulletin*, "MMR Vaccine—How Effective and How Safe?" April 2003. www.dtb.org.uk/dtb/news/pr/mmr.pdf.

For Further Reading

Books

Paul M. Ewald, *Evolution of Infectious Disease*. New York: Oxford University Press, 1996. This book discusses the evolution of disease-causing microbes. It includes information about treatment and transmission of diseases, and suggestions for making germs less deadly.

Mark Gladwin and Bill Trattler, *Clinical Microbiology Made Ridiculously Simple*. 3rd edition. Sydney: Medmaster, 2001. This book is a brief, clear treatment of clinical microbiology with information about bacteria, fungi, viruses, parasites, prions, and microbial resistance to medication.

John Postgate, *Microbes and Man*. 4th edition. Cambridge, England: Cambridge University Press, 2000. This accessible book contains information about microbes and their influence on humans and the environment.

Alvin Silverstein, Virginia Silverstein, and Robert Silverstein, *Measles and Rubella*. Berkeley Heights, NJ: Enslow, 1997. This book clearly explains the history, transmission, symptoms, and treatment of measles and rubella. It also includes an overview of vaccine development and examples of case studies and recent outbreaks.

June Thompson, *Spots, Birthmarks and Rashes*. London: Carroll & Brown, 2003. Written by a nurse, this book is a guide to childhood skin conditions, including noncontagious rashes, contagious rashes, insect bites, birthmarks, pigments, and growths.

Philip M. Tierno Jr., *The Secret Life of Germs: Observations and Lessons from a Microbe Hunter*. New York: Pocket Books, 2001. This book presents a wide-ranging discussion of disease-causing microbes, disease transmission, and germ warfare.

Works Consulted

Books

Paul R. Bloom and Paul-Henri Lambert, eds., *The Vaccine Book.* San Diego: Elsevier Science, 2003. This book contains extensive information about vaccines and diseases, including the cost and impact of immunization, microbial and parasitic diseases, development of new vaccines, economics of vaccines, and vaccine safety.

Randal G. Fisher and Thomas G. Boyce, *Moffet's Pediatric Infectious Diseases: A Problem-Oriented Approach.* 4th edition. Philadelphia: Lippincott Williams & Wilkins, 2004. This book provides a thorough discussion of childhood contagious diseases, including diagnosis and management of infectious diseases, syndromes associated with numerous organs and tissues, rash diseases, chronic illnesses, and congenital immunodeficiency syndromes.

Laurie Garrett, *The Coming Plague: Newly Emerging Diseases in a World Out of Balance.* New York: Farrar, Straus and Giroux, 1994. This book discusses the emergence and spread of deadly diseases. It includes information about attempts to eradicate diseases, newly emerged diseases, genetic engineering, urban centers of disease, drug-resistant microbes, and attempts to control contagious diseases.

Arno Karlen, *Man and Microbes: Disease and Plagues in History and Modern Times.* New York: Touchstone, 1995. This book contains an overview of the natural history of disease. It also presents and analyzes various plans for overcoming continuing public health crises around the world.

Ellen G. Strauss and James Strauss, *Viruses and Human Disease.* San Diego: Academic, 2002. This book provides extensive information about viruses, including a survey of viruses and viral infections, structure of viruses, RNA and DNA viruses, host defenses against viruses, and gene therapy.

Periodicals

S. Coughlan, J. Connell, B. Cohen, L. Jin, and H.W. Hall, "Suboptimal Measles-Mumps-Rubella Vaccination Coverage Facilitates an Imported Measles Outbreak in Ireland," *Clinical Infectious Diseases*, July 2002. www.ncbi.nlm.nih.gov/entrez/ query.fcgi?cmd=Retrieve&db=PubMed&list_uids=12060880& dopt=Abstract.

Jeffrey Cowley, "The Great Disease Migration," *Newsweek*, Fall/Winter 1991. www.millersv.edu/~columbus/data/art/ COWLEY01.ART.

Theresa Garner, "Rubella Outbreak Claims Three Children in Samoa," *The New Zealand Herald*, July 10, 2003. www.nzherald. co.nz/index.cfm?ObjectID=3527625.

Jia-Yee Lee and D. Scott Bowden, "Rubella Virus Replication and Links to Teratogenicity," *Clinical Microbiology Reviews*, October 2000. www.pubmedcentral.nih.gov/articlerender.fcgi?artid= 88950.

Jeanette Lloyd, "Learning About Congenital Rubella Syndrome," *National Parent Network Newsletter*, Winter 1992–1993, pp. 15–17.

Anita Manning, "A Booster Shot Against German Measles," *USA Today*, March 21, 2005. www.usatoday.com/news/health/ 2005-03-21-german-measles_x.htm.

Robert McCaa, "Spanish and Nahuatl Views on Smallpox and Demographic Catastrophe in the Conquest of Mexico," *Journal of Interdisciplinary History*, March 14, 1994. www.hist.umn. edu/~rmccaa/vircatas/vir6.htm.

Salvador Sandoval, "Human Epidemics Parallel the Course of Human Development," *People's Tribune*, October 2002. www.lrna.org/league/PT/PT.2002.10/PT.2002.10.4.html.

Sourav Sanyal, "Admn Readies to Tackle Measles Cases," *The Times of India*, February 19, 2004. http://timesofindia.india times.com/articleshow/505129.cms.

Time, "German Measles Menace," March 5, 1945. www.time.com/time/archive/preview/0,10987,797155,00.html.

———, "Measles," March 26, 1934. www.time.com/time/archive/preview/0,10987,747256,00.html.

David W. Tschanz, "The Arab Roots of European Medicine," *Saudi Aramco World*, 2004. www.saudiaramcoworld.com/issue/199703/the.arab.roots.of.european.medicine.htm.

Susan van den Hof, Christine M.A. Meffre, Marina A.E. Conynvan Spaendonck, Frits Woonink, Hester E. de Melker, and Rob S. van Binnendijk, "Measles Outbreak in a Community with Very Low Vaccine Coverage, the Netherlands," *Emerging Infectious Diseases*, June 2001. www.cdc.gov/ncidod/eid/vol7no3_supp/vandenhof.htm.

A.S. Weissfeld, W.D. Gehle, and A.C. Sonnenwirth, "Comparison of Several Test Systems Used for Determination of Rubella Immune Status," *Clinical Microbiology*, July 1982. www.pubmedcentral.nih.gov/pagerender.fcgi?artid=272298&pageindex=2#page.

Internet Sources

About Health and Fitness, "*Measles/Mumps/Rubella (MMR) Vaccine Information Statement*," 2005. http://pediatrics.about.com/cs/immunizations/ a/mmr_vis.htm?terms=measles.

Allina Hospitals and Clinics, "Vitamin A (Retinol)," April 2002. www.medformation.com/ac/CAM.nsf/conssupplements/VitaminARetinolcs.html.

Australian Broadcasting Company, "The Health Report: Rubella," June 23, 1997. www.abc.net.au/rn/talks/8.3./helthrpt/stories/s69.htm.

BBC News, "Measles Outbreak Feared," May 30, 2000. http://news.bbc.co.uk/1/hi/health/769381.stm.

———, "MMR Debate: Mothers' Stories," 2003. http://news.bbc.co.uk/1/hi/health/1113653.stm.

Brian Carnell, "Measles Outbreak in Great Britain," Overpopulation.com, February 18, 2002. www.overpopulation.com/articles/2002/000018.html.

David V. Cohn, "The Life and Times of Louis Pasteur," University of Louisville, February 11, 1996. www.louisville.edu/library/ekstrom/special/pasteur/cohn.html.

Felicity T. Cutts, Jennifer Best, Marilda M. Siqueira, Kristina En-
gstrom, and Susan E. Robertson, "Guidelines for Surveillance
of Congenital Rubella Syndrome and Rubella," Department of
Vaccines and Biologicals, World Health Organization, 1999.
www.who.int/vaccines-documents/DocsPDF99/www
9934.pdf.

Marie E. Daly, "Disease and Our Ancestors: Mortality in the
Eighteenth and Nineteenth Centuries," New England Historic
Genealogical Society, 2001–2005. www.newenglandances-
tors.org/education/articles/NEA/disease_and_our_ances
tors_mortality_in _the_eighte_607_1807.asp?print=1.

Benjamin Damien, "Design of an Immunization Strategy Based
on Recombinant Proteins of the Measles Virus in the Context
of a Changing Epidemiology," Laboratoire National de Santé
Université de Liége, Luxembourg, 2002. www.fundp.ac.be/
~bdamien/these-bdamien.pdf.

dr greene.com, "Fear, Measles, and Protecting our Kids," 2001.
www.drgreene.org/body.cfm?id=21&action=detail&ref=684.

Drug and Therapeutics Bulletin, "MMR Vaccine—How Effective
and How Safe?" April 2003. www.dtb.org.uk/dtb/news/pr/
mmr.pdf.

Miranda Eeles, "Iran Launches Mass Jab Campaign," *BBC News
World Edition.* December 6, 2003. http://news.bbc.co.uk/
2/hi/health/3296663.stm.

eMedicine: Consumer Health, "Skin Rashes in Children," 2004.
www. emedicinehealth.com/Articles/10189-1.asp.

Anthony S. Fauci, "A Commitment to Global Health," National
Institute of Allergy and Infectious Diseases, National Institutes of Health, 1999. www.niaid.nih.gov/director/usmed/
1999/usmed99text.htm.

Marilyn Fredrick, "One Mother's Story of Her Daughter with
CRS," Helen Keller National Center for Deaf-Blind Youths and
Adults, 1997. www.hknc.org/Rubella_One_Mothers_Story.
htm#Return%;20To%20Top.

Emir Emano Gamis, "Sorsogon Measles Outbreak Kills 11,"
Inq7.net, January 14, 2004. www.inq7.net/reg/2004/jan/14/
reg_5-1.htm.

Sharif Kaf Al-Ghazal, "The Valuable Contributions of Al-Razi (Rhazes) in the History of Pharmacy During the Middle Ages," Islamic Medicine online, 2002. www.islamicmedicine.org/al razi3.htm.

Health Professional's On-line Resource Centre, "Rubella Outbreak in the Pacific Islands," Immunisation Advisory Centre, University of Auckland, New Zealand, October 7, 2004. www.immune.org.nz/default.asp?a=625&t=561&View=Full Story&newsID=2.

Margaret Hunt, "Basic Virology: Replication of Viruses," Microbiology and Immunology On-line, 2004. www.med.sc.edu: 85/mhunt/replicat.htm.

David T. Imagawa, Pierre Goret, and John M. Adams, "Immunological Relationships of Measles, Distemper, and Rinderpest Viruses," Proceedings of the National Academy of Sciences of the United States of America, August 1960. www.pubmed central.nih.gov/articlerender.fcgi?artid=223010.

International Federation of Red Cross and Red Crescent Societies, "Measles in Africa," 2005. www.ifrc.org/WHAT/health/archi/fact/fmeasles.htm.

IRIN News.org, "Iran: Mammoth Vaccination Drive Will Benefit 33 Million," December 22, 2003. www.irinnews.org/report.asp?ReportID=38550&SelectRegion=Central_Asia&Select Country=IRAN.

KidsHealth. "Rubella (German Measles)," 2003. www.kids health.org/parent/infections/skin/german_measles.html.

March of Dimes News Desk, "March of Dimes Supports PAHO Effort to Eliminate Rubella," September 23, 2003. www.march ofdimes.com/printableArticles/9564_9803.asp.

Measles Initiative, "Largest Integrated Health Campaign Ever Saves Children from Africa's Two Leading Killers—Malaria and Measles," 2005. www.redcross.org/pressrelease/0,1077,0_ 314_4233,00.html.

Philip Minor, "Vaccine Protection Against Measles, Mumps and Rubella: Is There a Health Risk?" National Institute for Medical Research, 1998. www.nimr.mrc.ac.uk/MillHillEssays/ 1998/mmrcrohns.htm.

MMR—The Facts, "Statement on the Use of MMR Vaccine," January 24, 2001. www.mmrthefacts.nhs.uk/library/timeline.php?t=showall.

MMWR Weekly, "Measles Outbreak Among Internationally Adopted Children Arriving in the United States, February–March 2001," December 13, 2002. www.cdc.gov/mmwr/preview/mmwrhtml/mm5149a3.htm.

Kenneth Moss, "Measles Shots Are Common Sense: Personal Reflections of an Alaska Physician," Immunization Action Coalition, April 26, 2000. www.immunize.org/stories/story29.htm.

National Institutes of Health, "Measles," 2005. www.nlm.nih.gov/medlineplus/measles.html.

———, "Rubella," 2005. www.nlm.nih.gov/medlineplus/rubella.html.

Nancy O'Donnell, "A Report on a Survey of Late Emerging Manifestations of Congenital Rubella Syndrome," Helen Keller National Center, 1991. www.hknc.org/images/CRS_SURVEY 1991.htm.

Oregon Department of Human Services, "Measles (Rubeola)," 2004. www.dhs.state.or.us/publichealth/acd/measles/index.cfm.

Karen Pallarito, "Rubella No Longer a Threat in the U.S.," *Health-Day News,* March 21, 2005. www.healthday.com/view.cfm?id=524659.

Pan American Health, "Measles," 2005. www.paho.org/Pro ject.asp?SEL=TP&LNG=ENG&ID=112.

A. Rafila, M. Marin, A. Pistol, D. Nicolaiciuc, E.. Lupulescu, A. Uzicanin, and S. Reef, "A Large Rubella Outbreak, Romania—2003," Ministry of Health, Bucharest, Romania, National Center for Biotechnology Information, 2004. www.ncbi.nlm.nih.gov/entrez/query.fcgi?cmd=Retrieve&db=pubmed&dopt=Abstract&list_uids =15192257&itool=iconfft.

Reuters Health Information, "Infant Imports Measles, Causes Outbreak," January 22, 2004. www.ucsfhealth.org/childrens/cgi-bin/print.cgi.

S.E. Robertson, F.T. Cutts, R. Samuel, and J.L. Diaz-Ortega, "Control of Rubella and Congenital Rubella Syndrome (CRS) in Developing Countries, Part 2: Vaccination Against Rubella," *Bulletin of the World Health Organization*, 1997. www.who. int/vaccines-documents/DocsPDF/ww9656c.pdf.

Paul Roche, Jenean Spencer, Angela Merianos, "Editorial: Measles Elimination in Australia," Surveillance Section, Department of Health and Aged Care, Canberra ACT, August 2001. www.cda.gov.au/pubs/cdi/2001/cdi2503/pdf/cdi2503 m.pdf.

Alfred Sommer, "A Bridge Too Near," in *Nutrition: The Progress of Nations*, United Nations Children's Fund, 1995. www.unicef.org/pon95/nutr0002.html.

Julia Storm, "Rubella Outbreak—Arkansas, 1999," The Health Archives, University of Minnesota Extension Service, December 21, 2001. http://lists.extension.umn.edu/pipermail/health/2001-December/000466.html.

UCLA Library, "The UCLA Louise M. Darling Biomedical Library History and Special Collections Division Presents an Online Exhibit: Smallpox," 2000. www.library.ucla.edu/lib raries/biomed/smallpox/rhazes.html.

UNICEF, "Why Are Children Dying?" 2005. www.unicef.org/immunization/index_why.html.

World Health Organization, "Measles Deaths Drop Dramatically as Vaccine Reaches World's Poorest Children: Global Goal of Halving Measles Deaths Can Be Achieved," April 27, 2000. www.who.int/mediacentre/news/releases/2004/pr30/en/print.html.

Wrestling Legends.com, "Interview with the Legends: Benny McGuire," 2004. www.1wrestlinglegends.com/columns/inter views/inbm.htm.

A. Zahoor, "Abu Bakr Muhammad Bin Zakariya Ar-Razi (Rhazes)," Muslim Scientists in the Middle Ages, 1998. www.unhas.ac.id/~rhiza/saintis/razi.html.

Web Sites

Centers for Disease Control and Prevention (CDC) (www. cdc.gov). This Web site, run by the Centers for Disease Control and Prevention, has numerous links to articles and news stories about health issues. It includes information about prevention and control of infectious and chronic diseases, teen health, injuries, workplace hazards, disabilities, and environmental health threats. Photographs, charts, and maps illustrate many of the articles.

Medinfo (www.medinfo.co.uk). This Web site is run by Arboris medical services. It is written by a general practitioner in the United Kingdom and provides easy-to-understand information and advice about medical conditions, childhood ailments, immunizations, pharmaceuticals, medical tests, and other health issues. Some of the fact sheets contain illustrations.

MMR—The Facts (www.mmrthefacts.nhs.uk). This Web site is run by the Department of Health in London, England. It is designed to provide people with information about MMR vaccine so they can make informed decisions about inoculations. Users can visit an MMR library, ask an expert panel a question, learn about global use of MMR vaccine, and read recent news stories related to the vaccine. Links to maps and statistical charts are available.

National Foundation for Infectious Diseases (NFID) (www.nfid.org). The National Foundation for Infectious Diseases (NFID) is a nonprofit organization that encourages education about infectious diseases. The Web site contains fact sheets about contagious illnesses, scientific articles for health professionals, information about immunization, and links to additional health-oriented Web sites and to a virtual library of diseases. Many of the articles contain illustrations.

Index

Picture Credits

Cover image: Linda Stannard/Photo Researchers, Inc.
AP/Wide World Photos, 51, 55, 77
© Bettmann/CORBIS, 13, 17, 86
© Bill Varie/CORBIS, 24
Christine Nesbitt/EPA/Landov, 39
© David Turnley/CORBIS, 64
© Ed Lallo/ZUMA/CORBIS, 56
Hulton Archive/Getty Images, 83
© Hulton-Deutsch Collection/CORBIS, 20
Jan von Holleben/Getty Images, 40
© John Heseltine/CORBIS, 29
© Lester V. Bergman/CORBIS, 10 (background), 44, 47, 80
© Ludovic Maisant/CORBIS, 58
Maury Aaseng, 10, 31, 52
© N. Hashlamoun/Reuters/CORBIS, 88
© Najlah Feanny/CORBIS, 48
© Owen Franken/CORBIS, 36
Patrick Olum/Reuters/Landov, 93
© Royalty-Free/CORBIS, 9, 67, 75
Time Life Pictures/Getty Images, 23
© Tom Stewart/CORBIS, 71
Wolfgang Kumm/dpa/Landov, 62

About the Author

Barbara Saffer, a former college instructor, has PhD degrees in biology and geology. She grew up in New York City, has lived in Florida, Louisiana, Alabama, and Tennessee, and did research in many parts of the United States and Canada.

Saffer has written books about science, geography, exploration, famous people, and historical events, and her stories, articles, poems, and puzzles have appeared in numerous children's magazines. She has also written fun mystery books for children starring Shannon Holmes, private detective, and her parrot, Lucky. Barbara's other books in the Diseases and Disorders series are *Smallpox* and *Anthrax*.

Saffer lives in Chattanooga, Tennessee, with her husband, two children, and a variety of pets.